THE FEDERAL BUREAU OF INVESTIGATION'S
WEAPONS OF MASS DESTRUCTION COORDINATOR PROGRAM

EXECUTIVE SUMMARY

Chemical, biological, radiological, and nuclear weapons, also known as weapons of mass destruction (WMD), have the potential to kill thousands of people in a single attack. Although concern over WMDs is not new, the disastrous consequences that may result from using these weapons has spurred the federal government to prepare for and respond to WMD threats.

The Federal Bureau of Investigation (FBI) serves as the lead federal agency for investigating WMD crimes.[1] The FBI focuses its WMD-related activities towards preventing the illicit acquisition of WMDs and identifying and disrupting their attempted use. The preemptive focus of these efforts requires the FBI to use its investigative and analytical capabilities to identify potential WMD suspects, targets, and threats before an attack occurs.

Several different FBI investigative divisions once conducted WMD-related activities. In July 2006, the FBI consolidated its WMD investigation and prevention efforts into a WMD Directorate within its National Security Branch. Comprised primarily of Special Agents, Intelligence Analysts, program managers, and policy specialists, the WMD Directorate designs training for employees of the FBI; other federal agencies; state and local law enforcement organizations; and public health, industry, and academia partners. The WMD Directorate also provides national-level WMD intelligence support to FBI field divisions and to the larger U.S. Intelligence Community. At the local level, the FBI primarily relies on a designated Special Agent in each field division, referred to as the WMD Coordinator, to implement a significant portion of the FBI's WMD-related activities.

---

[1] The Attorney General has lead authority to investigate federal crimes, which includes the use or attempted use of a WMD. 28 U.S.C. § 533 (2008) and 18 U.S.C. § 2332(a) (2008). The Attorney General has delegated much of this investigative authority to the FBI. 28 C.F.R. § 0.85 (2008). The National Response Framework, prepared by the Department of Homeland Security and the National Implementation Plan, drafted by the National Counterterrorism Center, outline how federal agencies should work together to implement a broader strategy to detect, prevent, and deter WMD events.

OIG Audit Approach

The Department of Justice Office of the Inspector General (OIG) conducted this audit to: (1) assess how the FBI's WMD Coordinators should plan and perform activities that address prioritized WMD threats and vulnerabilities, (2) evaluate the FBI's integration of WMD Coordinator functions with field division intelligence capabilities and practices, and (3) review FBI efforts to ensure that WMD Coordinators and others that work on the WMD program have the skills and abilities necessary to detect and prevent WMD attacks.

In conducting this audit we interviewed over 80 FBI officials and employees, including the Assistant Director of the WMD Directorate. We conducted audit work at FBI headquarters in Washington, D.C., and at eight FBI field divisions: Houston, Texas; Oklahoma City, Oklahoma; Baltimore, Maryland; Washington, D.C.; New York, New York; Phoenix, Arizona; Tampa, Florida; and Los Angeles, California. We also attended an FBI WMD Coordinator training conference in Albuquerque, New Mexico presented by the WMD Directorate.

During this audit, we examined how the FBI supports and manages WMD Coordinators to enable them to address pressing WMD threats and vulnerabilities in their field divisions. We also reviewed how WMD Coordinators interacted with Intelligence Analysts and examined how they used information provided in WMD intelligence reports to enhance their knowledge of threats facing their field division. We further considered whether the FBI has provided adequate training for and oversight of its WMD Coordinator and Intelligence Analyst personnel. In addition, we examined WMD activity reports from each field division and reviewed strategic plans, operational guides, and FBI directives to ascertain WMD Directorate efforts to track and evaluate WMD Coordinator activities.

Appendix I includes additional details on the objectives, scope, and methodology of the audit.

Results in Brief

The FBI has begun using the concept of domain management to identify and prioritize the most significant WMD threats and vulnerabilities facing each of its field divisions.[2] WMD Coordinators serve as their field

---

[2] Domain management is the process by which WMD Coordinators work with their field division to obtain a strategic understanding, or domain awareness, of their area of responsibility by a continuous assessment of threats and vulnerabilities.

division's WMD subject matter experts. Nevertheless, for an internal FBI review, many WMD Coordinators could not identify the top, specific WMD threats and vulnerabilities that faced their particular field division. Recognizing that WMD Coordinators and their field divisions were not able to identify WMD threats consistently and completely, in September 2008 the FBI began requiring that its field divisions conduct an initial WMD domain assessment to help each division identify and prioritize WMD threats and vulnerabilities.

Despite serving as their field divisions' WMD subject matter experts, we found that WMD Coordinators have not participated directly on initial WMD domain assessments. Instead, Intelligence Analysts from field divisions' Field Intelligence Groups worked with the WMD Directorate at FBI headquarters to complete these assessments. Because domain assessments are necessary for WMD Coordinators to obtain a strategic understanding of WMD threats and vulnerabilities, we believe WMD Coordinators should participate in their field division's WMD domain assessment. Furthermore, because individuals conducting domain assessments need to be familiar with WMD-related information already obtained via FBI investigations, we believe that the FBI should require that: (1) its field divisions periodically review case files to identify and share WMD-related information with the WMD Coordinator and (2) Special Agents who work with outside companies and groups involved in WMD prevention and research share contact and outreach information with their WMD Coordinator.

In part to improve its information-sharing capabilities within the greater U.S. Intelligence Community, the FBI is in the process of implementing a new organizational framework and intelligence process to catalyze the production of timely and actionable intelligence reports. We found that the FBI has not formalized a method to facilitate collaboration between WMD Coordinators and Intelligence Analysts that ensures WMD Coordinators can fully use field division analytical capabilities to plan and perform their work. Furthermore, the FBI does not require its Field Intelligence Groups to designate specific Intelligence Analysts to work with WMD Coordinators. As a result of these issues, WMD Coordinators had limited or inconsistent interaction with their Field Intelligence Group, which has hindered them from fully applying intelligence to identify specific WMD threats facing their field division.

During the audit, officials with some Field Intelligence Groups told us that they were concerned that if Intelligence Analysts worked closely with WMD Coordinators, Intelligence Analysts would end up relegated to performing ancillary or administrative case duties such as following up with sources or electronically scanning documents. These officials believed that closer coordination between Intelligence Analysts and WMD Coordinators would risk reducing the time Intelligence Analysts would be able to devote to obtaining and reporting intelligence. Nevertheless, for the FBI to operate a continuous process for providing an ongoing flow of WMD intelligence, we believe that close interaction between WMD Coordinators and Intelligence Analysts is essential. Once Intelligence Analysts are designated to work with WMD Coordinators, the FBI should ensure that they are utilized appropriately to identify and assess WMD intelligence instead of being assigned to work on ancillary case duties.

We also found that the FBI has not established specific qualifications that WMD Coordinators need so that they can perform their critical functions. Additionally, the FBI has not formulated training plans to ensure that WMD Coordinators and WMD-assigned Intelligence Analysts acquire the skills necessary to manage their field division's WMD domain effectively. Although WMD Coordinators and Intelligence Analysts had received various types of WMD training, the training they received was not necessarily aligned with the threats and vulnerabilities that these personnel faced at the field division-level. We believe this was, in part, due to WMD Coordinators not being involved in the field division WMD domain assessment, as well as the FBI not adequately tracking the training received by its WMD field division personnel. Without requiring that WMD personnel complete specific WMD training and subsequently tracking its completion, the FBI is not positioned to identify and mitigate knowledge gaps in WMD preparedness.

In this report we make 13 recommendations relating to the FBI's WMD Coordinator program. These recommendations include implementing procedures to help increase WMD Coordinators' domain awareness, ensuring that WMD Coordinators and Intelligence Analysts are sharing WMD-related information, and providing the necessary training to ensure that WMD Coordinators and Intelligence Analysts have the skills necessary to address domain needs.

The remaining sections of this Executive Summary discuss in more detail our audit findings. Our report, along with the appendices, contains detailed information on the full results of our review of the FBI's WMD Coordinator program.

WMD Domain Management

Recognizing a need for a consistent mechanism that field divisions could use to perform activities aimed at preventing terrorist attacks, in June 2008 the FBI began to apply the "domain management" concept to guide and evaluate its field division WMD programs. As shown by the following exhibit, WMD domain management is a process by which WMD Coordinators and others continually identify, collect, and analyze information within their area of responsibility. Once collected, the information is assessed periodically to obtain a strategic understanding, or "domain awareness," of the most pressing WMD threats and vulnerabilities facing a field division.

DEPICTION OF A COMPREHENSIVE
WMD DOMAIN MANAGEMENT PROCESS

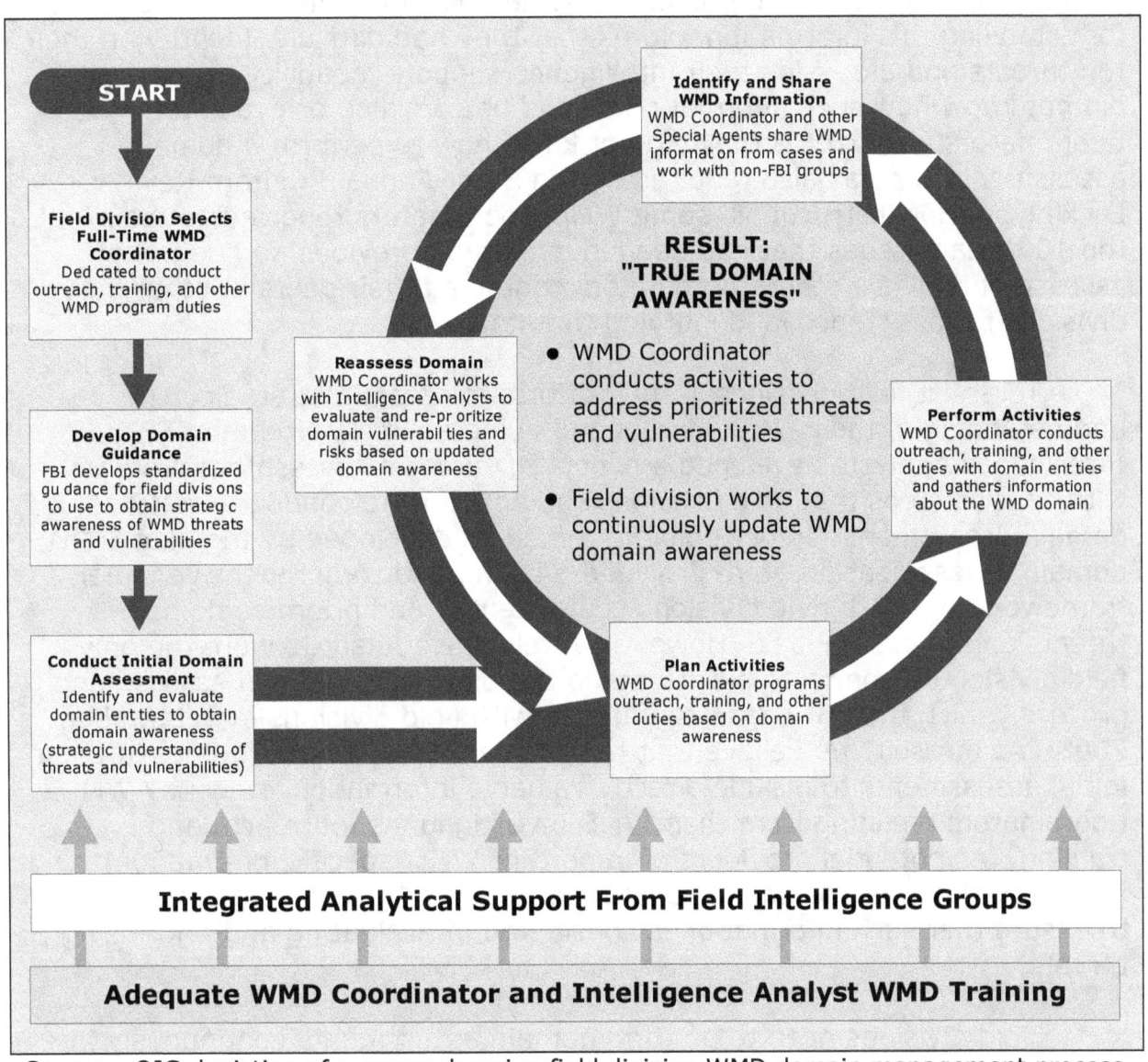

Source: OIG depiction of a comprehensive field division WMD domain management process

Continuous efforts to collect and assess information about domain entities are needed to achieve adequate domain awareness. As shown by the diagram above, a comprehensive domain management process requires support from field division intelligence groups and adequate training for

WMD Coordinators and Intelligence Analysts involved in the domain management process.

The FBI implemented the domain management process to guide its field division WMD programs in June 2008 as part of an internal Semi-Annual Program Review. As part of this review, each field division was asked to: (1) identify its "top 10" WMD threats, (2) assess its intelligence support capability, and (3) describe various training and outreach activities performed by the WMD Coordinator. Some WMD Coordinators responsible for compiling this information told us that they had difficulty identifying their top threats and assessing their intelligence support capability because they did not know how such information should be compiled or evaluated. WMD Coordinators also told us they did not know how to perform a domain assessment that was also required by the Semi-Annual Program Review. Lacking specific instructions, some WMD Coordinators reported as their top 10 threats issues that had been identified by previous ad hoc threat assessments, while other Coordinators contacted their peers at other field divisions for assistance in identifying threats.

To assist field divisions in their efforts to obtain a strategic understanding of their WMD threats and vulnerabilities, a team of FBI Intelligence Analysts developed a pilot WMD domain assessment program with specific steps that field divisions should follow to conduct a WMD domain assessment. In our opinion, the steps developed by the pilot WMD domain assessment program provided a useful and comprehensive initial framework by which field divisions could identify and prioritize domain threats and vulnerabilities. However, Intelligence Analysts were the only field division personnel to participate in the pilot WMD domain assessment process, which the FBI began conducting with field divisions in September 2008. As a result, we believe that the FBI has missed opportunities in these initial assessments to include directly valuable information known by WMD Coordinators resulting from their WMD investigations, outreach, and training. As potential providers of important WMD-specific information, WMD Coordinators should actively participate in future domain assessments to ensure that such information is considered in evaluating and prioritizing threats.

Field divisions need to perform domain assessments continuously in order to be aware of the constantly changing state of entities within the WMD domain and to share this information with the appropriate parties. It is therefore important that WMD Coordinators know WMD-related information acquired by other field division activities and personnel. For example, WMD connections may be uncovered by non-WMD investigations and other field division personnel, such as the Joint Terrorism Task Force

Coordinator, may obtain WMD-related information while working with local police departments. To ensure that WMD Coordinators are aware of such WMD connections, the FBI needs to require that field divisions establish standard procedures to identify and share all such information.

FBI efforts to track and oversee WMD Coordinator activities can also be improved. While the FBI WMD Directorate receives activity reports from WMD Coordinators that detail their training and outreach activities, WMD Coordinators do not submit such activity reports regularly. In addition, the activities detailed by WMD Coordinator on these reports do not specify how their activities target specific WMD domain threats or vulnerabilities facing their field division. To ensure that WMD Coordinators conduct training and perform other activities designed to address the threats and vulnerabilities prioritized for their domain, the WMD Directorate should require WMD Coordinators to submit activity reports regarding specific domain threats and vulnerabilities on a regular basis.

Intelligence Collaboration

In an effort to enhance its information-sharing capabilities within the larger U.S. Intelligence Community, the FBI has been implementing a new intelligence framework that realigns how it handles intelligence reporting. These intelligence initiatives have required active collaboration between various FBI programs, divisions, and personnel, including the FBI's Directorate of Intelligence, the WMD Directorate, and Field Intelligence Groups at each field division. Although these groups have been organized to work together in the prevention of WMD attacks, as shown by the exhibit below, the FBI has not provided a standard method by which WMD Coordinators and Field Intelligence Groups should share WMD intelligence at the field division level.

WMD PROGRAM INTELLIGENCE ORGANIZATION

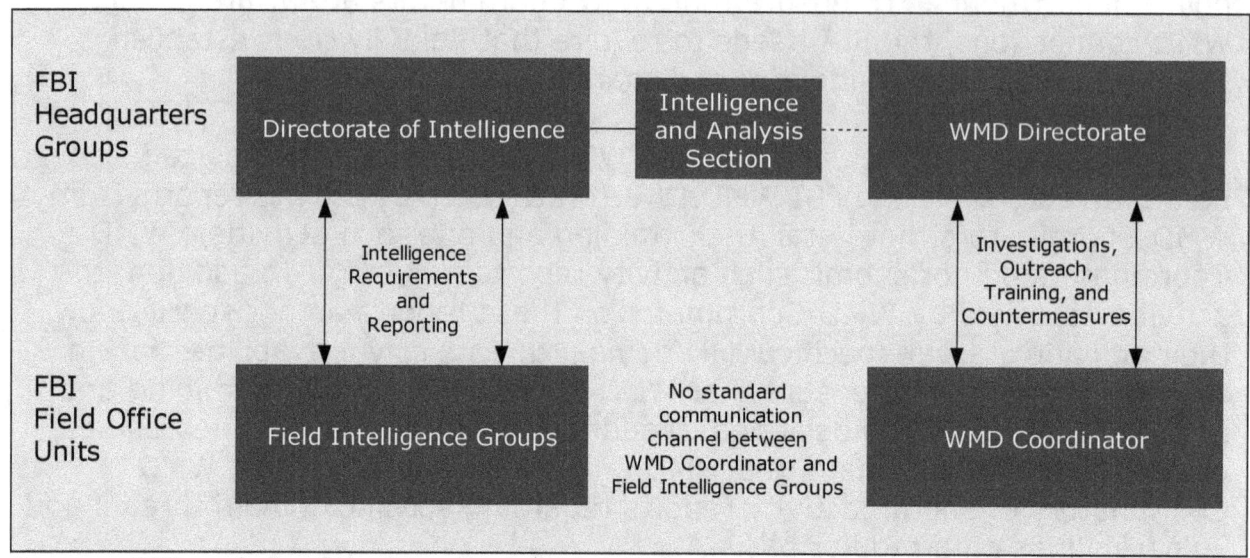

Source: OIG analysis of the Directorate of Intelligence and WMD Directorate

As the lead field division contact and subject matter expert on WMD matters, WMD Coordinators need to acquire and use WMD intelligence regularly to address prioritized domain needs. Although the FBI has been working to distinguish analytical responsibilities and eventually embed Intelligence Analysts in various tactical investigative squads, the FBI does not typically require field division Intelligence Analysts to work directly with the WMD Coordinator. As a result, WMD Coordinators reported that they had inconsistent interaction with field division Intelligence Analysts, which negatively affects their ability to identify and report WMD issues. We found that only 21 of 56 field divisions, or 38 percent, designated a specific Intelligence Analyst to work with the WMD Coordinator.

Field Intelligence Group officials and WMD Coordinators agreed that Intelligence Analysts and Special Agents do not always understand the approaches that each use to accomplish their work. WMD Coordinators and Special Agents who work with them focus on outreach and liaison activities that seek to prevent, prepare for, respond to, and contain terrorist acts. Intelligence Analysts spend much of their time evaluating raw or fragmented data and using their analysis to forecast potential threats facing their field divisions. We found some examples of WMD Coordinators collaborating with Intelligence Analysts to identify threats and vulnerabilities and other examples of Intelligence Analysts actively participating in WMD Coordinator outreach with important industry and law enforcement partners. However, some WMD Coordinators have only used analysts in ancillary roles, in part because some Field Intelligence Groups have been hesitant to designate specific Intelligence Analysts to work with WMD Coordinators. To some extent, this hesitation occurs because Intelligence Analysts and their supervisors perceive that they will be tasked with ancillary or administrative case duties, such as following up with sources or electronically scanning documents, rather than conducting research and gathering intelligence. Once the FBI designates Intelligence Analysts to work with WMD Coordinators, field divisions should ensure that these analysts are used appropriately.

WMD intelligence reporting is critical for identifying information needed to achieve WMD domain awareness. We reviewed the number of WMD intelligence reports issued by field divisions as reported in the June 2008 Semi-Annual Program Review and found that 30 out of 56 FBI field divisions did not disseminate any WMD intelligence products during this period. Meanwhile, only nine field divisions disseminated five or more WMD intelligence products. The field divisions that were able to disseminate the most WMD intelligence had an established approach to guide how their personnel handled intelligence reporting.

WMD Coordinator and Intelligence Analyst Training

The WMD Directorate is responsible for identifying, developing, and offering WMD training throughout the FBI. Since its inception in 2006, the WMD Directorate has increased the number of training courses and exercises offered to WMD Coordinators, other FBI Special Agents and Intelligence Analysts, and law enforcement personnel at federal, state, and local agencies. WMD Coordinators, in turn, are responsible for training other FBI Special Agents and field division personnel about detecting, handling, and responding to WMD threats. Because they serve as the field division's WMD subject matter expert and need to conduct activities to address domain needs, WMD Coordinators require specialized training on the highly technical nature of WMDs.

Field division managers are responsible for selecting Special Agents to be WMD Coordinators. However, the FBI has not issued written qualifications for the position, which has affected the WMD program in at least two ways. First, without knowing the specific skills and abilities required by the position, field division supervisors may not select the most qualified Special Agents as WMD Coordinators. Second, already designated WMD Coordinators may not know what additional training or skills they need to acquire to be an effective WMD Coordinator. Although formalized training plans could assist in ensuring that candidates become qualified for these positions, no such training plans exist. The FBI has begun to develop a WMD Coordinator certification program to aid in the development of WMD Coordinator knowledge and skills. However, the FBI has not yet implemented this program. Additionally, the FBI has not developed a WMD training plan for Intelligence Analysts who support WMD Coordinators.

We also found that the WMD Directorate lacked necessary mechanisms to track and report field division WMD training and, as a result, could not easily ascertain whether WMD Coordinators and Intelligence Analysts received adequate training. The FBI's Virtual Academy, the primary tool FBI personnel use to track training received, could only track FBI-provided training. Because FBI employees receive non-FBI WMD training that cannot be tracked by Virtual Academy, the WMD Directorate could not use Virtual Academy to ascertain the WMD training readiness of each field division. Consequently, in September 2008 the WMD Directorate began working with a contractor to expand and update another FBI training database called the Training Readiness Management System. WMD Directorate officials told us that once updated the database will provide them with the capability to track training received by WMD Coordinators, Intelligence Analysts, and non-FBI law enforcement and other WMD prevention and response partners. As planned, the updated database will also allow the WMD Directorate to identify training gaps and help FBI officials ascertain the level of WMD readiness at each field division.

However, our audit determined that once the Training Readiness Management System is updated, it will not interface with information contained in Virtual Academy. This means that to ensure the accuracy of the information contained in the different systems, the FBI will need to reconcile periodically the Training Readiness Management System with Virtual Academy. Such reconciliation, if performed at regular intervals, will ensure that both systems contain accurate information and potentially improve the reliability of the data used by the WMD Directorate to ascertain the WMD readiness of field division personnel.

Conclusions and Recommendations

Although the FBI began applying domain management to its field division WMD program in June 2008, it did not at this time provide WMD Coordinators the necessary guidance to identify and assess the top WMD threats and vulnerabilities within their respective field divisions. Lacking the ability to prioritize threats consistently, WMD Coordinators could not conduct outreach and plan training based on any concrete WMD-threat prioritization. Further, the WMD Directorate did not require that WMD Coordinators report their activities and training uniformly and therefore could not track what was reported to ensure that Coordinators were addressing the most important WMD domain threats and vulnerabilities.

The FBI also has not ensured that WMD Coordinators have sufficient analytical support. Because WMD intelligence is critical for identifying threats facing FBI field divisions, we found that WMD Coordinators require a more-structured intelligence apparatus to provide them with intelligence necessary to plan activities that address specific WMD threats. If Intelligence Analysts worked more closely with WMD Coordinators on WMD matters, these analysts would be better positioned to assist Coordinators in producing actionable WMD intelligence.

WMD Coordinators and Intelligence Analysts that work with them require specialized training on the highly technical nature of WMDs. The FBI has not implemented a formalized and required training program for these personnel. The FBI has also not established certain minimum qualifications for WMD Coordinators, and therefore some Coordinators had no background in WMD matters or had received only limited training before being named their field division's WMD Coordinator.

During this audit, the FBI and its WMD Directorate have taken steps to improve the field division WMD program. In addition to instituting the WMD domain management process, the WMD Directorate has implemented a full-time WMD Coordinator initiative and began to design a training plan for these critical WMD personnel. It has also taken steps to improve its training tracking system. Nevertheless, our report identified several areas that we believe need additional improvement. For example, the FBI should require that field divisions regularly review cases for WMD connections and share pertinent case information with appropriate personnel. The FBI should also regularly reconcile data in the Training Readiness Management System with Virtual Academy records.

Our audit contains 13 recommendations to improve and sustain the FBI's use of the WMD domain management process and ensure that WMD Coordinators have the resources and tools necessary to prevent and detect WMDs. Our audit recommends that the FBI:

- ensure that a WMD Coordinator or a designated assistant WMD Coordinator participates in the field division's WMD domain assessment,

- require that the WMD Directorate track WMD Coordinator activities against specific threats to ensure that each field division is adequately managing its WMD domain,

- require that each field division designate an Intelligence Analyst to meet with the WMD Coordinator periodically and discuss planned work and provide feedback on whether these activities will address prioritized domain needs,

- develop a method that reconciles Training Readiness Management System data with Virtual Academy records,

- finalize its WMD Coordinator certification program opportunities and ensure that the certification program offers threat-based courses based on the WMD domain threats and vulnerabilities within a WMD Coordinator's field division, and

- develop a targeted WMD training plan for Intelligence Analysts who work with WMD Coordinators that addresses the specific vulnerabilities and threats of the field division's WMD domain.

THE FEDERAL BUREAU OF INVESTIGATION'S WEAPONS OF MASS DESTRUCTION COORDINATOR PROGRAM

TABLE OF CONTENTS

INTRODUCTION

Chemical, biological, radiological, and nuclear weapons, also known as weapons of mass destruction (WMD), have the potential to kill thousands of people in a single attack. WMDs include any explosives and incendiary devices designed to cause death or serious bodily injury through the release, dissemination, or impact of toxic or poisonous chemicals, disease organisms, or radiation at a level dangerous to human life. If detonated or dispersed, WMDs may also persist in the environment and render entire cities uninhabitable for many years.

Although concern over WMDs is not new, the disastrous consequences that may result from a single WMD terrorist attack has spurred the federal government to prepare for and respond to WMD threats. The specific roles and responsibilities of various federal agencies to detect, mitigate, and prevent WMD attacks are outlined in two national-level documents: the National Response Framework (Framework) and the National Implementation Plan to Combat the War on Terror (National Implementation Plan). Together, these documents serve as a national WMD strategy to coordinate how various agencies work together to prevent and respond to WMD incidents.

The Federal Bureau of Investigation (FBI) serves an important role in addressing the threat of WMD, and is assigned as the lead federal agency for investigating WMD crimes.[3]

The National WMD Strategy

In January 2008, the Department of Homeland Security issued the National Response Framework to assign federal agencies specific responsibilities for preparing and responding to hazardous events. The Framework details the Attorney General's lead responsibility to investigate criminal and terrorist acts or threats and coordinate the activities of different law enforcement agencies. It also requires that federal government agencies, including the FBI, develop response plans, policies, and procedures on how they will provide resources and coordinate and carry out their response techniques. Under the Framework, agencies are also responsible

---

[3] The Attorney General has lead authority to investigate acts of federal crimes, including the use or attempted use of a WMD. See 28 U.S.C. § 533 (2008) and 18 U.S.C. § 2332(a) (2008). The Attorney General has delegated much of this investigative authority to the FBI. 28 C.F.R. 0.85 (2008). The National Response Framework and the National Implementation Plan do not alter any legally established responsibilities of the FBI or of other federal agencies. Instead these guidelines outline how federal agencies should work together to implement a broader strategy to detect, prevent, and deter WMD events.

for ensuring that all threat information is reported to and shared between different law enforcement organizations.

The National Implementation Plan, which was drafted by the National Counterterrorism Center in June 2006, defines the responsibilities of different federal agencies involved with preventing and responding to terrorist attacks.[4] The strategy outlined in this plan relies on three essential capabilities: (1) the ability to keep WMDs out of the hands of rogue nations and terrorists, (2) the ability to enlist and prepare our allies to combat terrorism, and (3) the ability to organize and prepare the United States to sustain its fight against terrorism.[5]

Several federal agencies have overlapping roles in controlling hazardous substances and preventing and responding to terrorist attacks. Recognizing that no single federal agency, regardless of its mission, possesses all the expertise and information necessary to identify, mitigate, and respond to all WMD events, the national WMD strategy delineates specific agency roles and responsibilities. Exhibit 1 lists the major responsibilities of agencies that play a pivotal role in this strategy.

EXHIBIT 1: FEDERAL AGENCY WMD RESPONSIBILITIES

Federal Agency	Responsibility
Department of Defense	Responds to domestic air incidents involving WMDs. Serves as the lead agency in international operations and nonproliferation efforts.
Department of Energy	Provides technical support on specialized assets, including nuclear and radiation threats. Maintains the Nuclear Emergency Support Team to assist other agency response and containment efforts.
Department of Homeland Security	Coordinates domestic security activities, including developing and maintaining a national WMD exercise program. Detects and warns of WMDs within the United States. Responds to domestic WMD incidents.
Department of State	Coordinates international WMD response, training efforts, and other activities.
Department of Justice	Investigates criminal and terrorist attempts to acquire and use WMDs. Collects, manages, and transports WMD crime scene evidence.

Source: OIG analysis of legislative and executive authorities

---

[4] The National Counterterrorism Center is a component of the Office of the Director of National Intelligence.

[5] To integrate and synchronize national counterterrorism and counterproliferation elements, the National Implementation Plan follows a strategic framework outlined in Homeland Security Presidential Directive 15, Annex 1 (June 29, 2006).

To help effectuate the National Implementation Plan, federal agencies also developed supporting plans outlining how they would perform their antiterrorism roles. The Department of Justice has designated the FBI as the primary lead for many of its WMD-related responsibilities outlined by the National Implementation Plan.

FBI Efforts to Implement Its WMD Mission

In October 2007, the FBI reported that it was investigating nearly 1,000 cases that involved WMD crimes, including attempted or actual WMD possession, threats, and hoaxes. To prevent WMD attacks, the FBI opens investigations to deter attempts of criminals and terrorists to obtain WMDs, and if their acquisition cannot be prevented, identify and disrupt any attempted WMD use. These cases require the FBI to use both its traditional investigative functions and its analytical capabilities to identify potential WMD suspects, targets, and other threats before they can coalesce and result in an attack.

As shown by Exhibit 2, FBI WMD activities involve headquarters divisions, such as the WMD Directorate and the Directorate of Intelligence, and field division personnel, including WMD Coordinators and Intelligence Analysts on Field Intelligence Groups.

EXHIBIT 2: KEY FBI GROUPS INVOLVED IN WMD DETECTION AND PREVENTION EFFORTS

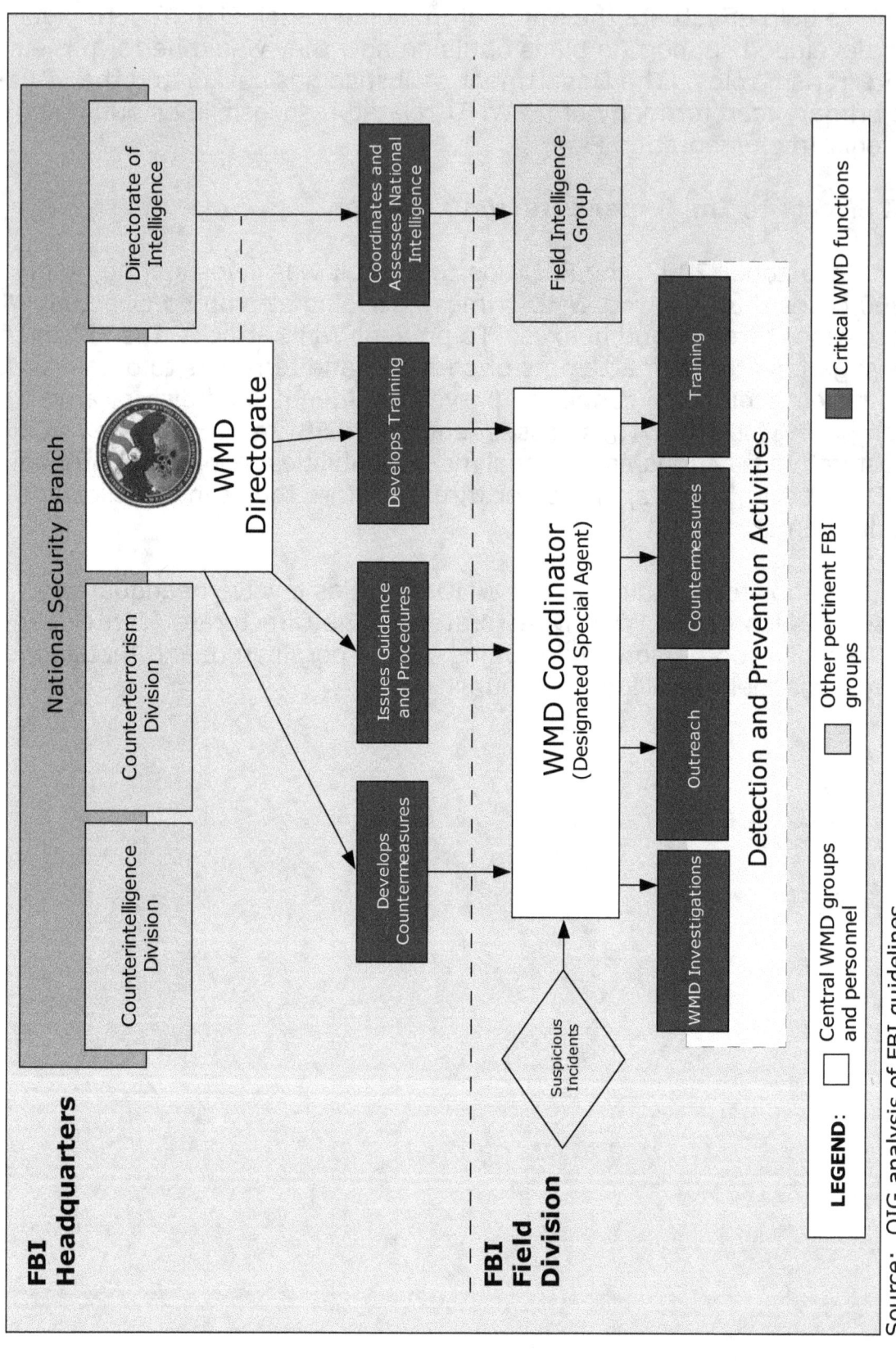

Source: OIG analysis of FBI guidelines

The WMD Directorate and its WMD Coordinators play a central role in the FBI's approach in addressing its WMD responsibilities. The WMD Directorate works with other FBI headquarters divisions to develop WMD program policies, training, and intelligence.[6] WMD Coordinators in the field divisions conduct WMD investigations and perform outreach and awareness training to those involved in handling WMD material throughout their regions. WMD Coordinators also institute countermeasures designed to prevent and detect WMD threats and attacks within their area of responsibility or domain.

WMD Directorate

Various WMD prevention and response efforts were once conducted by different FBI investigative divisions. In July 2006, the FBI consolidated its WMD-related activities into a single WMD Directorate within its then newly formed National Security Branch.[7]

Comprised primarily of Special Agents, Intelligence Analysts, program managers, and other policy specialists, the WMD Directorate designs training for employees of the FBI; other federal agencies; state and local law enforcement organizations; and public health, industry, and academia partners. The WMD Directorate also provides national-level WMD intelligence support to other intelligence agencies and develops initiatives, referred to as "countermeasures," that help reveal, interrupt, or destabilize terrorist efforts to use WMDs. Led by an Assistant Director, the WMD Directorate includes three sections, as shown in Exhibit 3: Countermeasures and Preparedness, Investigations and Operations, and Intelligence and Analysis.

---

[6] The FBI has established several distinct investigative programs at its headquarters and field divisions. The FBI bases its investigative programs on criminal and national security priorities such as counterterrorism, counterintelligence, cyber crime, violent crime, organized crime, and WMD.

[7] Designed to combine the intelligence, counterterrorism, and counterintelligence capabilities of the FBI, the National Security Branch unifies the FBI's counterterrorism-related activities.

EXHIBIT 3: THE WMD DIRECTORATE

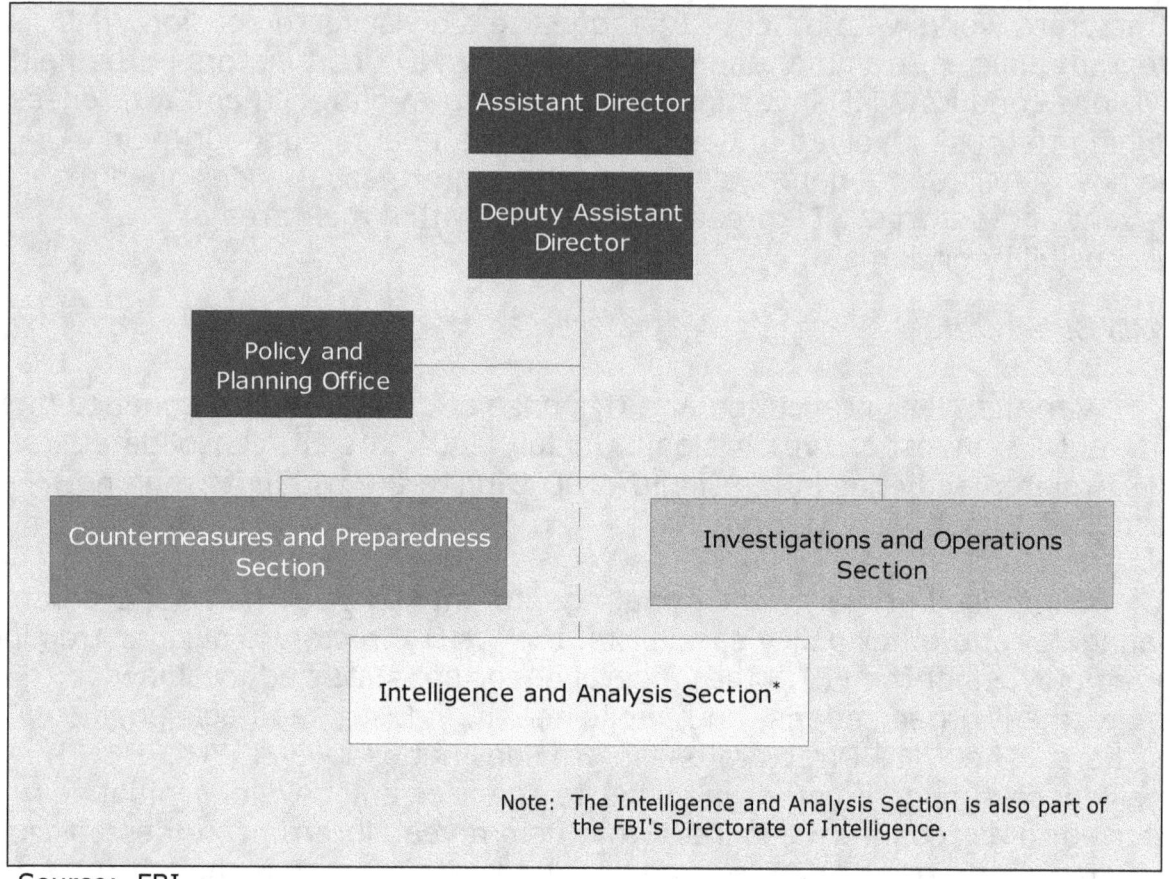

Note: The Intelligence and Analysis Section is also part of the FBI's Directorate of Intelligence.

Source: FBI

The WMD Directorate's Countermeasures and Preparedness Section develops initiatives and investigative tools to identify and disrupt potential WMD threats and attacks, prepares the FBI to respond to such events, and initiates and participates in domestic and international preparedness exercises. The Investigations and Operations Section includes the WMD Operations Unit (Operations Unit) and the Counterproliferation Operations Unit. The Operations Unit manages cases and daily threat calls and serves as the WMD Directorate's primary conduit to WMD Coordinators in the field divisions while the Counterproliferation Operations Unit works with the Counterintelligence and Counterterrorism Divisions to identify WMD links in new and ongoing investigations.

The Intelligence and Analysis Section is a Directorate of Intelligence section embedded within the WMD Directorate.[8] Its Intelligence Analysts

---

[8] The FBI's Directorate of Intelligence manages all FBI intelligence activities. The Directorate of Intelligence is responsible for ensuring that intelligence is identified, collected, analyzed, and communicated in accordance with U.S. Intelligence Community standards.

identify threat patterns and sources and assess the tactics and capabilities of investigative targets. This section also coordinates, shares, and produces WMD intelligence products that focus on international and national-level WMD threats, including proliferation and terrorism.

WMD Coordinators

The FBI relies on a designated Special Agent at each field division, referred to as the WMD Coordinator, to implement a significant portion of its WMD-related activities. WMD Coordinators have been a part of the FBI since the mid-1990s when its WMD Operations Unit, which was then a part of the Counterterrorism Division, asked each field division to appoint a Special Agent to be a WMD Coordinator.

Some field divisions have assigned additional FBI personnel to assist their WMD Coordinator. For example, several field divisions have backup or assistant WMD Coordinators who help with outreach and evidence gathering tasks. Intelligence Analysts and technically trained Special Agents in the field also provide analysis and tactical support on WMD investigations. In addition, each field division may also have several other coordinators and personnel that play a role in the field division's WMD Program, including the Hazardous Materials Response Team Leader, the Special Agent Bomb Technician, the Domain Management Coordinator, the Counterproliferation Coordinator, and the Infragard Coordinator. These employees often perform outreach and community liaison tasks, which is also one of the key functions of the WMD Coordinator.

WMD Coordinator Responsibilities and Activities

Initially, FBI field divisions treated the WMD Coordinator position as a collateral duty, which entailed serving as a "point person" for suspicious WMD incidents. Each field division also had wide discretion over who to designate as the WMD Coordinator and what duties they were to perform. Over time, however, the FBI WMD Operations Unit provided field divisions with additional guidance and oversight in an effort to formalize the role of the WMD Coordinator position in each field division.[9] For example, in April 2008, the Operations Unit asked field divisions to designate WMD Coordinators as a full-time duty due to the large volume of work they managed. To encourage field divisions to designate a full-time WMD Coordinator, the WMD Directorate offered many field divisions a

---

[9] Besides the National Implementation Plan, specific National Security Presidential Directives (NSPDs) and Homeland Security Presidential Directives (HSPDs) have clarified the FBI's role in WMD and other counterterrorism and intelligence collection efforts.

headquarters-funded position to replace the one filled by the full-time WMD Coordinator.

The role of WMD Coordinators has also evolved over time to become the field division's "subject matter expert" on WMDs. In April 2008, the WMD Directorate issued a memorandum detailing specific WMD Coordinator responsibilities, as shown in Exhibit 4.

EXHIBIT 4: WMD COORDINATOR RESPONSIBILITIES

1. **Conduct Outreach.** Establish and maintain strong operational and intelligence-focused relationships with federal, state, and local counterparts, including private industry, academic institutions, and other entities involved in manufacturing or safeguarding WMDs or WMD delivery systems.

2. **Investigate WMD Crimes.** Conduct and assist in investigations of WMD crimes and subjects, including other types of criminal and terrorism cases that involve WMDs.

3. **Implement Countermeasures.** Implement initiatives designed by FBI headquarters, specifically the WMD Directorate, to detect and deter specific WMD threats and vulnerabilities. Develop and test ways to reveal and mitigate WMD risks and report results to FBI headquarters.

4. **Provide Training.** Teach WMD prevention, awareness, and detection techniques to pertinent representatives in the field division, both within the FBI and the public community.

5. **Manage Incident Response.** Serve as the subject matter expert in areas of chemical, biological, radiological, and nuclear (CBRN) incidents. Apply CBRN knowledge to assess and address WMD incidents and threats reported to the field division.

Source: FBI WMD Directorate

In addition to the responsibilities outlined above, WMD Coordinators must also know about and be up-to-date on issues pertaining to WMDs that are in their field division's geographic area of responsibility. Such issues include: (1) the sources for WMD materials within their geographic area of responsibility; (2) how and where hazardous materials are transported; (3) where hazardous materials are stored; (4) the security vulnerabilities of the locations holding hazardous materials; and (5) the locations of various companies or groups including research reactors, medical waste producers, chemical facilities, and biological laboratories.

WMD Coordinators are also the public face of the FBI's WMD program within each field division and are responsible for liaison activities such as:

- Training. WMD Coordinators plan, host, and attend training sessions for groups within their field division's area of responsibility, ranging from informal discussions with manufacturers and industry leaders to multi-day field division exercises with local first responders that generate "after-action" reports detailing lessons learned.

- Outreach. WMD Coordinators routinely work with other agencies and organizations such as the Department of Energy, the Department of Homeland Security, and state and local emergency and public health departments. Outreach performed by WMD Coordinators also encapsulates a number of different activities, ranging from making telephone calls to attending local Department of Homeland Security Biowatch Program meetings.[10] Additionally, WMD Coordinators meet with academic groups and scientific institutions to obtain information about potential WMD hazards and share awareness about the FBI's role in investigating WMD crimes.

- Countermeasures. WMD Coordinators also deploy countermeasure initiatives developed by the WMD Directorate to address specific national threats and concerns. These countermeasures range from simple "meet and greets" at hardware stores to a comprehensive evaluation of security measures at small airfields across the United States.

As a result of their work with non-FBI groups, WMD Coordinators constitute an important source of intelligence on threats and vulnerabilities. Several FBI officials noted that WMD Coordinators often work with their field division's counterterrorism and counterintelligence squads to provide insight and assistance in identifying WMD links in new and ongoing cases.

---

[10] The Department of Homeland Security's Biowatch Program is an early warning system that can detect trace amounts of biological materials that can be the result of a terrorist attack. A Biowatch Program is administered in several major cities.

OIG Audit Approach

The Department of Justice Office of the Inspector General (OIG) conducted this audit to: (1) assess how the FBI's WMD Coordinators should plan and perform activities that address prioritized WMD threats and vulnerabilities, (2) evaluate the FBI's integration of WMD Coordinator functions with field division intelligence capabilities and practices, and (3) review FBI efforts to ensure that WMD Coordinators and others that work on the WMD program have the skills and abilities necessary to detect and prevent WMD attacks. To accomplish these objectives, we:

- examined how the FBI supports and manages WMD Coordinators so that they can address the most pressing WMD threats and vulnerabilities in their field divisions,

- reviewed how WMD Coordinators interact with Intelligence Analysts, and

- assessed whether the FBI provided adequate guidance on what skills and abilities WMD Coordinators should have and reviewed WMD Coordinator and Intelligence Analyst training opportunities and oversight to determine whether the FBI ensures that these personnel can perform essential WMD functions.

We conducted audit work at FBI headquarters in Washington, D.C., and at eight FBI field divisions: Houston, Texas; Oklahoma City, Oklahoma; Baltimore, Maryland; Washington, D.C.; New York, New York; Phoenix, Arizona; Tampa, Florida; and Los Angeles, California. We selected these field divisions based on a methodology that considered various aspects of field division WMD activities, intelligence and operational capabilities, and geographic size and location. In addition, we examined WMD activity reports from each field division and reviewed intelligence reports, strategic plans, operational guides, and FBI directives. We also attended and evaluated an FBI WMD Coordinator training conference provided by the WMD Directorate in Albuquerque, New Mexico.

The Findings and Recommendations section details the audit results. Appendix I includes additional details on the audit objectives, scope, and methodology.

FINDINGS AND RECOMMENDATIONS

I. WMD COORDINATORS NEED TO PARTICIPATE IN THE WMD DOMAIN MANAGEMENT PROCESS TO ADDRESS WMD THREATS AND VULNERABILITIES

Despite serving as their field division WMD subject matter experts, WMD Coordinators do not participate in the domain assessments that the FBI has begun using to identify and prioritize the WMD threats and vulnerabilities facing each of its 56 field divisions. Instead, the FBI has generally relied only on its Intelligence Analysts to assess WMD domains, which we believe may lead to incomplete domain assessments that do not fully consider important domain entity information obtained and known by WMD Coordinators. The FBI also does not have standard procedures for its field divisions to ensure that WMD case information and liaison contacts are identified and shared with WMD Coordinators. Further, the FBI needs to (1) enhance its WMD Coordinator oversight efforts and (2) improve performance evaluation criteria to ensure WMD Coordinators perform activities that address prioritized WMD threats and vulnerabilities.

In fulfilling the FBI's mission to detect and prevent WMD attacks, WMD Coordinators serve as their field division's primary representative to public- and private-sector groups that trade and develop material that can be used to manufacture WMDs. As the field division subject matter expert on WMD issues, WMD Coordinators need to work with other groups to identify and help prioritize the most serious WMD threats and vulnerabilities facing their geographic regions.

Recognizing a need for a consistent mechanism that field divisions could use to plan and perform activities geared toward preventing terrorist attacks, in June 2008 the FBI began to apply the "domain management" concept to guide and evaluate its major programs. Domain management is the process by which field division investigative programs continually collect and analyze information within their respective area of responsibility to obtain a strategic understanding of their most pressing threats and vulnerabilities. Once a program's threats and vulnerabilities are prioritized, Special Agents and other personnel working on the investigative program should accomplish activities that address the prioritized concerns and weaknesses. By working to detect and prevent specific types of crimes before they occur, effective domain management should help the FBI in its efforts to prevent a WMD attack.[11]

WMD Domain

The FBI's WMD domain constitutes a broad range of elements within a field division's area of responsibility. These elements, referred to as "domain entities," include anything that has the potential to create, transport, or use WMDs. Domain entities may also be any building, individual, or location that terrorists could target with a WMD attack. Exhibit 5 provides examples of various entities constituting a field division's WMD domain.

---

[11] Throughout the audit, the methods by which field divisions evaluated and performed their WMD program activities changed in response to the FBI's implementation of domain management. Recognizing these changes, we adjusted our audit objectives during our review to ensure that we assessed how the FBI's application of domain management to field division WMD programs would affect the WMD Coordinator's role. We then used the results of our fieldwork to determine what we believe are best practices that the FBI needs to implement to sustain a comprehensive WMD domain management process at its field divisions. Because the FBI only began to apply the domain concept to its field division WMD programs during our audit, we could not evaluate the results of its implementation of the domain management process.

EXHIBIT 5: EXAMPLES OF WMD DOMAIN ENTITIES

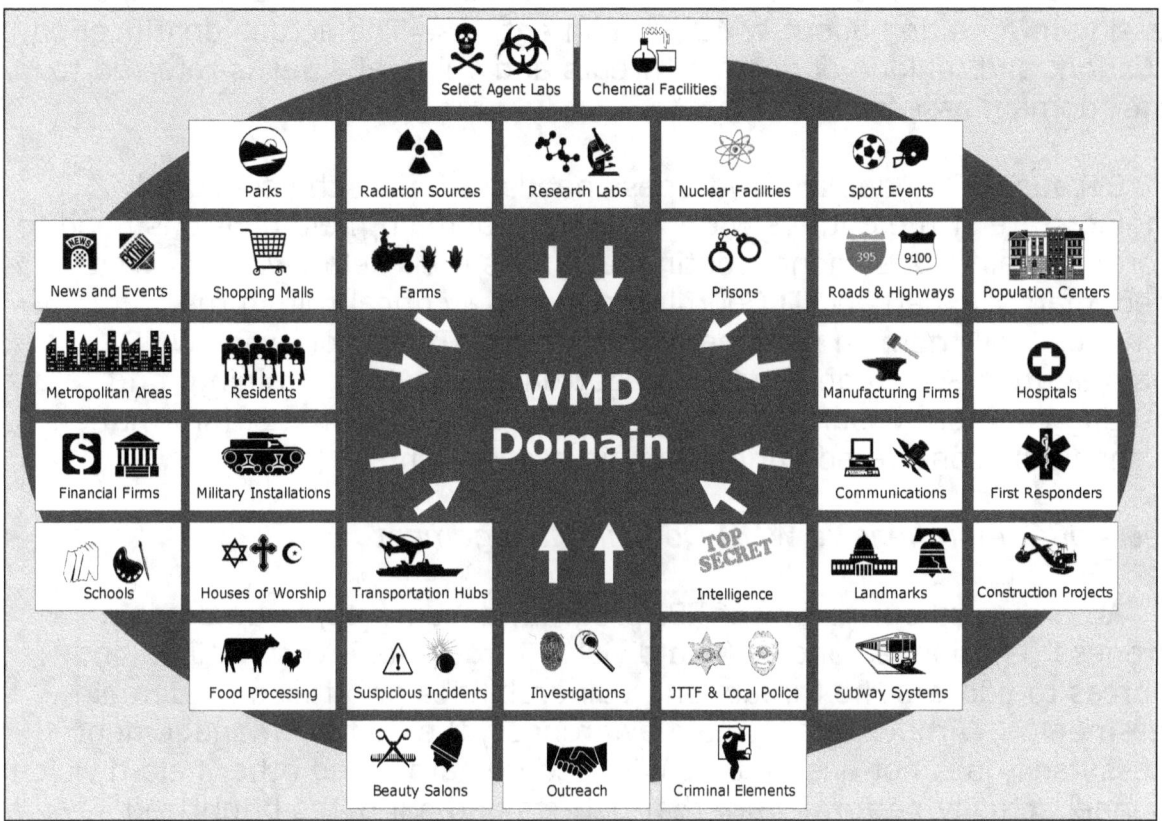

Source: OIG depiction of examples of WMD domain entities as conveyed by WMD Directorate officials, WMD Coordinators, and other FBI documents

As shown by Exhibit 5, the WMD domain encompasses the people, places, and things within a field division's geographic area of responsibility. It includes various types of FBI and non-FBI entities. FBI WMD domain entities include prior and ongoing investigations, sources, reports of suspicious incidents and threats, and intelligence. Non-FBI WMD domain entities include both public and private sector interests such as transportation hubs, nuclear power plants, laboratories, hospitals, manufacturing firms, and shopping malls. Because field divisions cover distinct geographical areas and these areas contain different domain entities, each field division's WMD domain is unique.

Domain Management

A field division's WMD domain can include thousands – if not millions – of different entities. It is therefore not feasible for field divisions to assess the threats and vulnerabilities presented by all domain entities simultaneously. The WMD domain management process requires that field divisions acquire a strategic understanding of the most serious threats and vulnerabilities of their field division's WMD domain. This strategic understanding, referred to as "domain awareness," requires collecting and assessing information about WMD domain entities. The actual identification, evaluation, and ranking of domain threats and vulnerabilities is referred to as the "domain assessment."

Because WMD domain awareness needs to reflect the constantly changing state of the entities within the WMD domain, field divisions need to perform domain assessments continuously. As their field division's WMD subject matter expert, WMD Coordinators play a critical role in the continuous WMD domain management process. Their work with WMD domain entities – through conducting outreach, providing training, and instituting countermeasures – provides an important source of information that should be considered during domain assessments.

Aspects of Comprehensive WMD Domain Management

According to our review of FBI program documents, "true domain awareness" is achieved once a field division targets its investigations and resources to address the threats and vulnerabilities prioritized by domain assessments. Without true domain awareness, the domain management process itself does not ensure that WMD Coordinators and other field division personnel actually perform work that detects and mitigates prioritized threats and vulnerabilities. For instance, consider that a field division's WMD domain assessment revealed a nuclear power plant lacks adequate safeguards over its fuel rod storage tank. In this example, for the field division to achieve true domain awareness the field division would need to ensure that its WMD Coordinator both planned and performed specific activities to address the domain vulnerability of weak fuel rod security. Such activities may include meeting with plant representatives to discuss their security needs or providing plant managers with WMD awareness training. Conversely, if the assessment revealed a potential attack against a nuclear power plant, to achieve true domain awareness the WMD Coordinator would need to perform specific activities geared toward mitigating that threat. These activities may include beginning investigations on the potential attackers, increasing the plant's security, and notifying local law enforcement of the threat made against the plant. In both examples, the results of the WMD Coordinator's efforts would need to be tracked so that subsequent domain assessments result in accurate domain awareness.

These examples illustrate that a comprehensive WMD domain management process needs to do much more than identify and prioritize threats and vulnerabilities before "true domain awareness" may be achieved. Specifically for the FBI's WMD efforts, domain management should be viewed as a continual process for understanding the dynamic nature of WMD threats and vulnerabilities. Exhibit 6 illustrates how domain assessments and activities could work together on a field division WMD domain management process that detects and prevents WMD attacks.

EXHIBIT 6: DEPICTION OF A COMPREHENSIVE WMD DOMAIN MANAGEMENT PROCESS

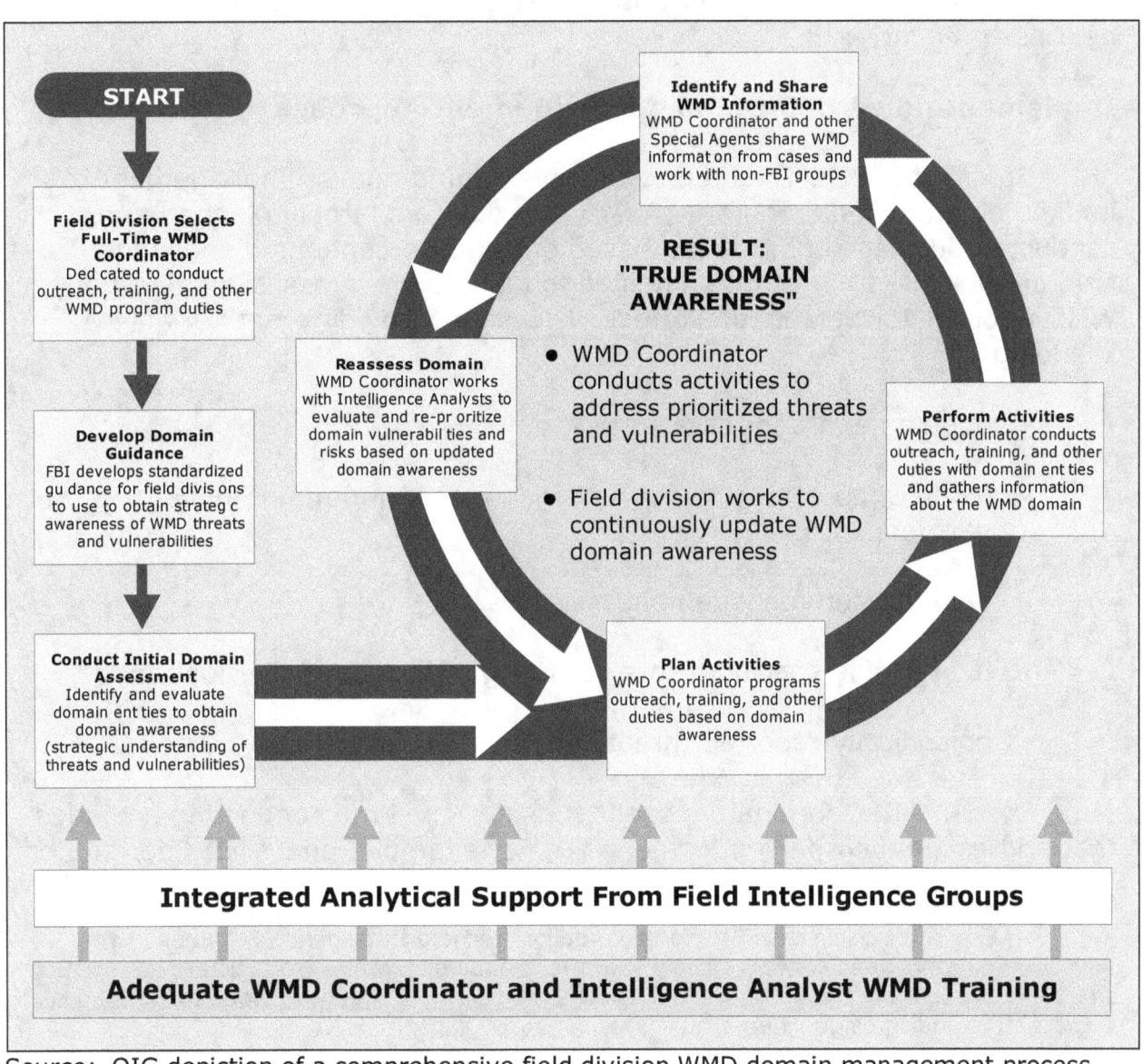

Source: OIG depiction of a comprehensive field division WMD domain management process that results in "true domain awareness"

Because domain management is driven by how field divisions obtain and process information, we believe that WMD Coordinators and others working in the WMD domain need to: (1) be supported by and integrated with field division analytical capabilities, such as the Field Intelligence Group, so that information on threats and vulnerabilities can be evaluated quickly and accurately; and (2) receive sufficient training so that they can adequately assess WMD threats and respond to WMD incidents.[12]

With sufficient intelligence and training support, WMD domain management applies updated domain assessment results to plan and perform activities that mitigate prioritized threats and vulnerabilities and acquire new WMD domain information that should then be evaluated by the next assessment.

Implementing a WMD Domain Management Approach

Before the WMD Directorate began applying domain management to its field division WMD programs, WMD Coordinators largely planned and conducted outreach and training based on their perceptions of individual field division risks.[13] Without any standardized domain assessments, many WMD Coordinator perceptions of risk were shaped by different variables, including:

- ongoing and prior casework,

- established contacts with first responders and major industry partners,

- field division management concerns,

- high-profile special events occurring in their field division, and

- episodically reported threats and weaknesses.

Some WMD Coordinators spent considerable time conducting activities that addressed their perceptions of risk. For example, one WMD Coordinator

---

[12] Finding II discusses FBI efforts to realign its Field Intelligence Groups and why WMD Coordinators need to work closely with these analytical groups to facilitate information sharing and intelligence reporting. Finding III assesses the training provided to WMD Coordinators and Intelligence Analysts.

[13] As discussed in the Introduction, WMD Coordinators also implement countermeasures to address WMD specific threats and vulnerabilities. However, many such countermeasures have been developed by the WMD Directorate and are based on detecting and mitigating threats and vulnerabilities based on international and national-level analysis and trend forecasting. WMD Coordinators are assigned to perform these countermeasures by the WMD Directorate. As such, we do not consider countermeasures to be specific, domain-based activities that the WMD Coordinator can plan and perform to address prioritized threats and vulnerabilities in their field divisions.

16

was performing a substantial amount of outreach and WMD awareness training with livestock producers. Another WMD Coordinator told us they spent significant time interacting with representatives from oil refineries. Although these groups represented a major industry in each field division's respective area of responsibility, WMD Coordinator efforts with these industries were based primarily on the WMD Coordinator's perception of risk that a WMD attack might occur, or the detrimental effect that such an attack would have on these industries and the WMD Coordinator's field division. For example, livestock may be purposefully contaminated with pathogens that would result in a poisoned food supply and endanger the health of millions. Similarly, chemicals stored by oil companies could explode and create plumes of toxic gas and poison the environment.

Regardless of the potential impact a WMD attack on these industries might have, without a domain assessment WMD Coordinators cannot ensure that their outreach and training efforts actually addressed the most critical threats and vulnerabilities within their field division's area of responsibility. Recognizing this weakness, the FBI has begun to take steps to implement a comprehensive WMD domain management process. As discussed previously, the WMD Directorate has asked field divisions to designate full-time WMD Coordinators, and during our audit has also begun: (1) introducing and detailing what domain awareness is to its field divisions and (2) conducting initial domain assessments using field division Intelligence Analysts.

June 2008 Semi-Annual Program Review

The FBI began applying domain management to field division WMD programs in June 2008 as part of its WMD Semi-Annual Program Review.[14] The WMD Directorate, working with the FBI's Inspection Division, formulated the questions and metrics that the WMD Semi-Annual Program Review needed to capture from each field division. Field divisions also received a form on which it was to report this information to FBI headquarters.

The WMD Semi-Annual Program Review outlined the major aspects of the domain management process and emphasized the importance of

---

[14] The WMD Semi-Annual Program Review was part of a larger FBI initiative that began in 2008 to replace the FBI's traditional 3-year field division inspection cycle with a performance measurement-based assessment process. The first FBI-wide Semi-Annual Program Review was started in June 2008 by the FBI Inspection Division. It gathered and evaluated information from major FBI investigative programs. WMD Semi-Annual Program Review results were received by FBI headquarters in August 2008. The review covered the period beginning October 1, 2007, and ending June 30, 2008.

continuously performing domain assessments. It also instructed field divisions to perform initial domain assessments based on the threats and vulnerabilities indicated by ongoing WMD program activities and investigative priorities. However, the WMD Semi-Annual Program Review did not detail how field divisions or their WMD Coordinators and Intelligence Analysts should determine and prioritize WMD domain threats and vulnerabilities. The WMD Semi-Annual Program Review instead had each field division: (1) identify its "top 10" WMD threats, (2) assess its intelligence support capability, and (3) describe various training and outreach activities performed by the WMD Coordinator.

Some WMD Coordinators responsible for compiling this information told us that they had difficulty identifying their top threats and assessing their intelligence support capability because no one told them how this information should be compiled or assessed. WMD Coordinators also told us they did not know how to perform an initial domain assessment that the Semi-Annual Program Review indicated was required to begin managing the WMD domain. Without detailed instructions, some WMD Coordinators reported as their top 10 threats those that had been identified by previous ad hoc threat assessments, while others contacted different field divisions or WMD Directorate officials for assistance in identifying threats.

Without clear guidance, field divisions and their WMD Coordinators were unable to identify WMD threats and vulnerabilities consistently if at all. For example, some field divisions listed 10 specific WMD threats that included the location of nuclear reactors, the names of particular biological and chemical manufacturers, WMD research facilities, and chemical weapons storage sites. Other field division lists did not include any such details. One field division listed broad threats such as "chemicals" or "biological agents." Three field divisions did not report any WMD threats.

September 2008 Pilot WMD Domain Assessment Program

The inconsistent June 2008 Semi-Annual Program Review results demonstrated that field divisions were not applying uniform approaches to assess their WMD domain threats and vulnerabilities. To address this problem, the FBI directed a team of Intelligence Analysts to develop a pilot WMD domain assessment program with specific steps that field divisions should follow to conduct a domain assessment.

In our opinion, the steps developed by the pilot WMD domain assessment program provide a useful and comprehensive initial framework by which field divisions can identify and prioritize domain threats and vulnerabilities. The assessment steps require that field divisions identify specific domain entities and listed examples of some non-obvious WMD domain entities that should be considered while evaluating domain threats and vulnerabilities. Examples of such entities include commercial centers, companies receiving chemical and biological research grants and contracts, and colleges and universities.

Once the template WMD domain assessment program was compiled by the end of September 2008, the FBI began using it to assess each field division's domain for the subsequent WMD Semi-Annual Program Review. To prepare each field division for the next round of review, field divisions sent Intelligence Analysts to FBI headquarters to work with the WMD Directorate and the Directorate of Intelligence to complete their respective field division's initial WMD domain assessment. At FBI headquarters, these analysts identified case information and used intelligence reports to compile the initial assessment.

However, Intelligence Analysts were the only field division representatives that participated directly in the WMD domain assessment performed at FBI headquarters. While intelligence plays a pivotal role in identifying WMD domain threats and vulnerabilities, intelligence reports are not the only source of information that domain assessments need to gauge WMD domain threats and vulnerabilities adequately. Our fieldwork revealed that WMD Coordinators across different field divisions maintained different working relationships with Intelligence Analysts. Some WMD Coordinators worked closely with designated Intelligence Analysts and shared information about WMD threats with them regularly. WMD Coordinators at other field divisions did not routinely interact with Intelligence Analysts.

However, even in cases where WMD Coordinators have a close working relationship with an Intelligence Analyst, that Intelligence Analyst may not be the same one that conducts the WMD domain assessment. Therefore, if WMD Coordinators do not participate in some direct way on the assessment, important information stemming from their work on WMD investigations, outreach, and training may not be evaluated by the analyst conducting the assessment. As a result, the threats and vulnerabilities identified by a domain assessment conducted only by Intelligence Analysts may not capture the threats and vulnerabilities offered by some domain entities of which the WMD Coordinator has knowledge. These domain assessments therefore risk resulting in incomplete domain awareness that does not adequately prioritize all actual WMD threats and vulnerabilities. Without ensuring that all pertinent domain entities are considered in the WMD domain assessment, the FBI does not do all it can to help its WMD Coordinators detect and prevent the most probable WMD attacks.

Therefore, we recommend that the FBI ensure that a WMD Coordinator or a designated assistant WMD Coordinator participates in their field division's WMD domain assessment. Such participation should offer WMD Coordinators or their designees an opportunity to provide their view of pressing WMD matters, report on the status and results of their outreach and training efforts, and exchange pertinent WMD information with Intelligence Analysts also working on the domain assessment.

Identifying and Sharing WMD Information from Case Files and Outreach Activity

To participate meaningfully in the domain management process, WMD Coordinators need to know what information the FBI already has about the WMD domain. FBI cases and outreach activities can serve as major operational sources of WMD domain information. Case files can include background material on subjects that possess WMD capabilities and information on terrorist or other criminal enterprises that have been attempting to acquire WMDs. Additionally, some field divisions have assigned personnel other than WMD Coordinators to work with non-FBI agencies and groups, such as chemical and technology development groups, which may also serve as WMD domain entities. Consequently, we believe it is important that the FBI ensure that field divisions identify and share WMD domain information available from case files and other Special Agents with the WMD Coordinator.

WMD Information from Investigation Case Files

Both new and ongoing investigations are important WMD domain information sources. Because field divisions manage thousands of ongoing cases and are continually beginning new investigations, one aspect of a comprehensive domain management process should include identifying potential WMD connections or links in the constantly changing FBI investigation universe. However, because of the way the FBI classifies and administers its cases, more effort is required to identify and share WMD connections in cases that have not been classified as WMD investigations.[15]

---

[15] Appendix II contains additional details on FBI's case classification system.

The WMD Directorate and WMD Coordinators in the field divisions manage and participate on cases classified as "WMD investigations." WMD Coordinators play a direct role in these investigations, which is summarized in Exhibit 7. As a result, WMD Coordinators have access to pertinent information derived from cases classified as WMD investigations. The WMD Coordinator can then assess such case information while managing the WMD domain.

EXHIBIT 7: SUMMARY OF TYPES OF WMD INVESTIGATIONS

Domestic Police Cooperation. Efforts to assist local and state law enforcement agencies to target and mitigate WMD threats and vulnerabilities.

Atomic Energy Act Violations. The Atomic Energy Act guides the civilian and military development, access, and use of nuclear materials, called restricted data. These cases investigate alleged or suspected communication, receipt, or tampering of restricted data.

Other Federal WMD Violations. Investigating the actual or attempted use, possession, transfer, production, or transportation of chemical, biological, radiological, and other types of devices under 18 U.S.C. § 2332(a).

Counterproliferation. These cases include efforts to proactively monitor, detect, and prevent malicious subjects from even acquiring WMDs or mitigating the effects of a WMD event.

Preparedness. Activities to enhance how the FBI and other domain entities respond to a WMD or other hazardous event.

Source: OIG analysis of WMD-categorized FBI investigations

FBI divisions also conduct other types of cases that can potentially include WMD connections even though they are not classified as "WMD cases." For example, the Counterterrorism Division manages domestic and international terrorism cases. Some of these cases may include suspects or targets that have the ability, desire, or means to acquire and deploy a WMD device. Because WMD Coordinators do not participate directly on these investigations, the Counterterrorism Division needs to notify the WMD Coordinator directly – or indirectly via the WMD Directorate – of a WMD link in its cases so the WMD Coordinator can assess and address potential WMD vulnerabilities or risks stemming from the connection.

We found that field division counterterrorism squads have periodically provided information on WMD connections in their investigations to WMD Coordinators. In addition to identifying WMD connections in ongoing cases, some smaller field divisions have begun notifying WMD Coordinators whenever they begin a new counterterrorism case. However, field divisions have not established standard procedures to ensure that pertinent case information about WMDs is identified and then shared with WMD Coordinators.

Without systemic efforts to identify and share WMD connections in cases, WMD Coordinators may not be aware of all the entities within their WMD domains. This lack of information can affect the quality of the WMD domain assessment and WMD Coordinator's ability to prioritize activities that address the most serious threats and vulnerabilities. As part of its domain assessment initiative, during our audit the WMD Directorate recognized this deficiency and had field division Intelligence Analysts begin "scrubbing," or comprehensively reviewing, selected cases to identify WMD links. Although this effort may be able to identify WMD connections in prior or ongoing cases at the field division level, such activities should be periodically performed to ensure that domain assessments timely consider WMD connections that arise from new and updated case information.

During the audit, the WMD Directorate began working with the FBI's Counterterrorism Division to identify WMD connections in international terrorism cases. This ongoing effort includes dedicating six WMD Directorate personnel to the Counterterrorism Division's International Terrorism Operations Sections. In addition, the WMD Directorate has also worked with the Counterterrorism Division to create case file templates for Special Agents to consider when they conduct their investigations in domestic and international terrorism cases. According to Directorate personnel, the templates will help remind Special Agents of issues they may encounter that indicate a WMD connection. For example, the proposed template will include background on the types of academic degrees required to produce WMDs. Special Agents can then use the case file template as a reference source to identify potential WMD links in their investigations and as a reminder to refer this information to the WMD Coordinator.[16]

---

[16] We also found that some field divisions, namely the Houston and Oklahoma City field divisions, have begun using a similar case file template approach on their own in an attempt to identify potential WMD connections within their cases.

The Intelligence Analyst case review and the WMD Directorate initiatives with the Counterterrorism Division are important but preliminary steps that the FBI has undertaken to identify and share WMD connections in its new and ongoing investigations. The FBI still needs to ensure that WMD connection checks occur regularly to reveal relevant developments or changes in cases involving WMDs. These connections need to then be provided to the WMD Coordinator so they can be included and evaluated by the domain assessment. Therefore, we recommend that the FBI develop procedures to ensure that field divisions regularly: (1) review cases for WMD connections, and (2) share pertinent case information with appropriate personnel so it can be evaluated during WMD domain assessments.

WMD Information from Other Special Agents Working With Non-FBI Groups

In addition to a WMD Coordinator, each field division has designated Special Agents who routinely interact with non-FBI agencies and groups to support certain aspects of their respective FBI program activities, as shown in Exhibit 8. In some cases, the non-FBI groups that these agents meet with are also WMD entities and therefore are integral parts of a field division's WMD domain.

EXHIBIT 8: OTHER FIELD DIVISION PERSONNEL PERFORMING OUTREACH

Designated Special Agent Position	Primary Outside Groups Targeted	Primary Collaboration Goals
Counterproliferation Coordinator	Businesses, Export Violation Operations Centers	Obtain a "big picture" perspective of counterproliferation trends or threats, inform non-FBI assets on what to be prepared for on a day-to-day basis, and identify possible counterproliferation methods and issues.
Counterintelligence Domain Coordinators	Academic Institutions and Private Industries, especially financial and government contractors	Cooperate with financial and business sector to obtain and share sensitive information and data that could affect their operations and businesses.
Hazardous Material (HAZMAT) Team Leader	Downrange Operators	Increase the awareness of hazardous materials and ensure proper evidence collection and handling of evidence.
Special Agent Bomb Technician	State and Local Law Enforcement Agencies and Emergency Responders	Identify, respond to, and render safe explosive devices.
Joint Terrorism Task Force (JTTF) Coordinator	State and Local Law Enforcement Agencies	Share intelligence and other national security information with other law enforcement groups.

Source: OIG analysis of field division coordinator activities and responsibilities

The FBI is also involved in a wide array of industrial, scientific, and academic working groups, ranging from small regional banking associations to large international chemical research consortiums. To facilitate this involvement, the FBI assigns agents and analysts to attend working group meetings and speak to working group members. While performing this work, FBI personnel establish contacts and meet with representatives from multiple companies, research laboratories, and universities – all of which again are entities within the WMD domain.

We discussed with WMD Coordinators the type of information that these Special Agents can acquire from working with outside groups. A significant amount of information related to domain entities that otherwise would not be readily available can be obtained from this work, including the following:

- the organizational structure and key leaders of the group;

- contact telephone numbers and e-mail addresses of group officials, and other contact information that may be needed in an emergency;

- observational notes, such as whether the outside group employs rigorous security procedures or safeguards potentially hazardous materials;

- whether the outside groups are aware of the FBI's role in detecting and mitigating WMD events; and

- whether members of the outside group have been receptive to or cooperative with FBI outreach efforts.

In view of the nature of information that can be obtained, FBI personnel interacting routinely with non-FBI groups that are WMD domain entities constitute important sources of WMD domain information. Nevertheless, our audit did not identify any field division that clearly specified how WMD Coordinators and other personnel who routinely worked with non-FBI organizations and groups should share information. In fact, some WMD Coordinators said that they did not share information on their liaison contacts with other Special Agents and, in turn, other Special Agents did not share such information with them. Some WMD Coordinators also stated that they were reluctant to share liaison contact information because they wanted to remain their field division's primary point of contact with non-FBI groups. As a result, WMD Coordinators maintained their outside contact lists on their cell phones, Blackberry devices, and laptops, and did not always keep updated paper copies and make this information readily available to other field division personnel.

The lack of rigorous information sharing between FBI personnel working with outside groups means that WMD Coordinators may not obtain all the information the FBI possesses on WMD domain entities. In addition to affecting the ability of the WMD Coordinator to plan and prioritize their WMD domain activities, the lack of information sharing may affect the overall ability of the field division to respond to a WMD emergency. For example, if WMD Coordinators do not provide their field divisions with copies of their contact records prior to leaving the office, field divisions may not be able to contact quickly the non-FBI individuals or groups that had worked with the WMD Coordinator to begin investigating the threat.

We found that the lack of information sharing also resulted in different FBI personnel contacting the same groups for similar reasons. In these cases, FBI personnel did not know that another FBI official was already working with the outside company or group – which ended up confusing outside contacts. In an effort to address these occurrences and improve the efficiency of outreach efforts, the Counterintelligence Division uses a Domain Liaison Knowledgebase for its field division squads to use. The database allows counterintelligence agents and analysts to record, track, and share points of contact and other outreach-related information statistics.

In late 2008, FBI intelligence officials began working with the Counterintelligence Division to expand the use of the Domain Liaison Knowledgebase with other FBI divisions, including the WMD Directorate and its WMD Coordinators. Once fully implemented, we believe that the database will help prevent duplication of effort among field division personnel who work with outside groups. We recommend that the FBI continue its efforts to enhance the sharing of WMD domain entity information acquired by personnel working with outside groups. In our opinion, these efforts should: (1) identify the personnel who regularly work with non-FBI groups that are WMD domain entities; and (2) require that these personnel and the WMD Coordinator exchange pertinent WMD domain entity information using the Domain Liaison Knowledgebase.

Enhancing WMD Coordinator Oversight and Guidance

A comprehensive WMD domain management process requires that WMD Coordinators use domain awareness to plan and perform activities that address prioritized threats and vulnerabilities. As discussed previously, the WMD domain includes many entities, such as hazardous chemical facilities, manufacturing firms, and nuclear power plants. In addition, domain entities also involve "lone wolves" or rogue or extremist individuals threatening to carry out WMD attacks. Because WMD Coordinators must address both known and unknown domain threats and vulnerabilities, we believe they require significant oversight. The following sections provide two examples of how the FBI can increase WMD Coordinator oversight and guidance to help them work within the domain management process to prevent WMD attacks.

Tracking WMD Coordinator Activities That Address Domain Needs

Before the advent of the domain management process, WMD Coordinators were largely planning outreach and training efforts based on perceived risks of a WMD attack. Because there were no consistent and up-to-date assessments of threats and vulnerabilities facing their entire field division, WMD Coordinators had limited means to identify these WMD risks and plan activities that addressed them. Instead, many WMD Coordinators we spoke to relied on already-established contacts and suggestions from other field division WMD Coordinators to determine what activities they could perform.

Considering the various methods WMD Coordinators used to identify and schedule their activities in the absence of domain management guidance, we believe that, under a domain management process, WMD Coordinators need to receive guidance on how they should plan and conduct activities. While the pilot WMD domain assessment program we described earlier has provided some needed written guidance for field divisions to uniformly assess WMD threats and vulnerabilities, we concluded that the FBI needs to increase its overall oversight and tracking of WMD Coordinator activities.

The WMD Directorate is in a unique position to provide additional oversight to WMD Coordinators at each field division. It has worked with field divisions on their initial domain assessment and already receives a list of each field division's top vulnerabilities and threats via the WMD program Semi-Annual Program Review. In addition, the WMD Directorate receives summaries of WMD Coordinator activities because WMD Coordinators have been required to report periodically their field division activities using a standard FBI statistical accomplishment report form, which provides a blank area that WMD Coordinators use to describe their work performed, such as training and outreach.[17]

To increase WMD Coordinator oversight, we believe the WMD Directorate can use the Semi-Annual Program Reviews and activity reports to obtain and track the following information for each WMD Coordinator:

- the activities WMD Coordinators are performing in their field divisions,

- whether WMD Coordinator activities are planned to address a specific and prioritized domain threat and vulnerability, and

- whether these activities, once they were performed, actually addressed the prioritized WMD domain threat and vulnerability.

Moreover, although activity reports provide an overview of WMD Coordinator work, the way each WMD Coordinator reports activities has not been standardized. The level of detail provided by the activity reports varies considerably, and they do not always indicate why WMD Coordinators performed specific activities or whether these activities actually addressed threats and vulnerabilities. Furthermore, the WMD Directorate has not required that WMD Coordinators regularly submit activity reports. As a result, some WMD Coordinators submitted activity reports once a week or after completing major activities, while others submitted activity reports sporadically or when prompted by the WMD Directorate. Therefore, to ensure consistent and timely reporting of WMD Coordinator activities, we recommend that the FBI ensure that WMD Coordinators submit activity reports at regular intervals to facilitate tracking activities against domain needs.

Once the WMD Directorate obtains activity report data, it can compare the activities WMD Coordinators performed to the top threats reported by each field division. This comparison could provide the WMD Directorate with the information to assess whether WMD Coordinators focused on detecting

---

[17] The WMD Directorate uses the activity reports to compile statistics for internal FBI and congressional data requests. In June 2008, the WMD Directorate announced that it had begun revamping both the method and form that WMD Coordinators use to report their activities. Activity reports will be submitted via an electronic communication. Instead of having one large blank narrative area, the new format has 10 specific categories of activities: (1) prevent and detect, (2) investigations, (3) special projects, (4) intelligence, (5) planning, (6) liaison, (7) training received, (8) training provided, (9) intra-agency coordination, and (10) inter-agency coordination.

and mitigating their field division's prioritized threats and vulnerabilities. This information would also allow the WMD Directorate to identify the field divisions that require assistance to keep their WMD domain management processes on track. Without this information, the WMD Directorate may not know whether a field division is having difficulty using domain awareness to prioritize its WMD prevention efforts.

As a result, we recommend that the FBI require that the WMD Directorate track WMD Coordinator activities against specific WMD domain threats and vulnerabilities to ensure that each field division is adequately managing its WMD domain. This type of tracking will provide the WMD Directorate with the information necessary for it to: (1) ascertain periodically whether each WMD Coordinator is adequately addressing reported domain threats and vulnerabilities while performing field division activities; and (2) provide guidance, when necessary, to WMD Coordinators and their supervisors when WMD Coordinator activities are not addressing WMD domain threats and vulnerabilities.

Measuring WMD Coordinator Performance on Domain Activities

The FBI maintains a performance plan system that rates each employee against established critical elements determined by specific job functions. For example, FBI Special Agents are rated against a set of performance measures specific to the Special Agent position. While WMD Coordinators are Special Agents, the WMD Coordinator position is full-time with distinct responsibilities. Presently, the FBI uses Special Agent critical elements, such as investigative accomplishments and human source development, to rate the performance of WMD Coordinators. However, under the domain management approach, WMD Coordinators need to focus on managing the WMD domain and performing activities based on domain awareness. As a result, their duties do not align with general Special Agent performance elements.

To ensure that WMD Coordinators focus on applying domain awareness to plan and accomplish activities that address prioritized domain needs, we believe that WMD Coordinator performance should not be based solely on the Special Agent critical elements. For example, a WMD Coordinator may choose to conduct outreach or teach an entity based on the number of potential sources at that entity because that has been identified as a priority for Special Agents, instead of based on whether that entity constitutes a prioritized domain threat or vulnerability. Although domain management may impact investigations and develop potential sources, a more accurate performance-rating plan should be based on how the WMD Coordinators address their domain management needs. Therefore, we recommend that the FBI develop performance-rating plans for the WMD Coordinator position based on the tasks and skills necessary to manage the WMD domain effectively.

Conclusion

The FBI has begun to use domain management to administer and evaluate field division WMD programs, which can identify and prioritize their WMD threats and vulnerabilities. Because field divisions were not able to identify WMD threats and vulnerabilities consistently in the first WMD Semi-Annual Program Review, the FBI subsequently began conducting an initial domain assessment with each field division. However, we found that these initial domain assessments were being conducted not with WMD Coordinators, but rather with field division Intelligence Analysts.

Domain assessments lacking active participation from WMD Coordinators are potentially inadequate for two reasons. First, WMD Coordinators are the field division's subject matter expert on WMDs. They are charged with performing outreach and training individuals and groups about WMD awareness, detection, risk mitigation, and response. Without participating in the WMD domain assessment, WMD Coordinators may not know how to best plan their outreach and training to address their field division's prioritized threats and vulnerabilities. Second, WMD Coordinators are also a valuable source of WMD domain information. We believe that their information should be made readily available during the domain assessment process, and we recommend that WMD Coordinators participate in their field division's domain assessments.

In our opinion, the advent of domain management should not significantly change the function of the WMD Coordinator. Domain management should instead change how WMD Coordinators prioritize, plan, and report their activities. Before domain management, WMD Coordinators applied various perceptions of risk to decide what WMD training and outreach to perform. Under domain management, using perceptions of risk will no longer suffice because WMD Coordinators will need to plan activities that address specific needs and weaknesses identified during the domain assessment. To facilitate the ability of the WMD Coordinator to acquire the information for continuous domain assessments, the FBI needs to improve how WMD Coordinators and other Special Agents share WMD information. In addition, the FBI should conduct periodic reviews of its case files to identify WMD connections and ensure that employees who perform work with outside agencies share WMD relevant information with the WMD Coordinator. We believe that both of these activities will increase the availability of operationally derived information and help domain assessments provide a more accurate strategic understanding of WMD domain threats and vulnerabilities.

The FBI needs to ensure that WMD Coordinators plan and conduct activities based on domain awareness. To accomplish this, the WMD Directorate should also track WMD Coordinator activities against their field division's prioritized threats and vulnerabilities and assess WMD Coordinator performance based on how they plan and perform activities that address WMD domain needs.

Recommendations

We recommend that the FBI:

1. Ensure that a WMD Coordinator or a designated assistant WMD Coordinator participates in their field division's WMD domain assessment.

2. Develop procedures to ensure that field divisions regularly: (1) review cases for WMD connections and (2) share pertinent case information with appropriate personnel so it can be evaluated during WMD domain assessments.

3. Enhance the sharing of WMD domain entity information acquired by personnel working with outside groups.

4. Ensure that WMD Coordinators submit activity reports at regular intervals to facilitate tracking activities against domain needs.

5. Require that the WMD Directorate track WMD Coordinator activities against specific WMD domain threats and vulnerabilities to ensure that each field division is adequately managing its WMD domain.

6. Develop performance-rating plans for the WMD Coordinator position based on the tasks and skills necessary to manage the WMD domain effectively.

II. WMD COORDINATORS REQUIRE CLOSE COLLABORATION WITH DESIGNATED INTELLIGENCE ANALYSTS TO FACILITATE WMD INTELLIGENCE COLLECTION AND REPORTING

Despite efforts to realign WMD investigations with field division intelligence capabilities, the FBI has not designated specific Intelligence Analysts to work with WMD Coordinators to facilitate WMD intelligence sharing. Intelligence Analysts skilled in WMD can provide complex assessments and help WMD Coordinators draft intelligence reports concerning intelligence trends, leading to expanded WMD Coordinator domain awareness. Additionally, although the WMD Directorate acquires and shares intelligence resources with the Directorate of Intelligence and its Field Intelligence Groups, the WMD Coordinator is not a formal part of the FBI's intelligence process. As a result, the FBI has not ensured that WMD Coordinators are consistently applying intelligence resources to detect and mitigate WMD threats and vulnerabilities.

Intelligence collection is a major priority for FBI field divisions. In testimony provided to the House Judiciary Committee on September 2008, FBI Director Robert Mueller stated that, "intelligence gathering does not happen at Headquarters, it happens out in the communities [the FBI] serves." The FBI's Strategic Plan acknowledges that one of the largest challenges facing the FBI is establishing a common approach for collecting and assessing intelligence. Because WMD Coordinators collect information as part of their operational responsibilities and Intelligence Analysts assess information with their Field Intelligence Groups, we believe that WMD Coordinators and Intelligence Analysts need to work together better to facilitate intelligence collection and evaluation within the WMD domain management process.

Overview of FBI Intelligence Cycle

As discussed in Finding I, intelligence is an integral WMD domain entity. In gathering, sharing, and assessing intelligence, the FBI uses a decentralized approach to identify emerging WMD threats. This intelligence cycle, shown in Exhibit 9, involves many processes and steps that require collaboration between participating programs and divisions. The FBI's intelligence cycle seeks to resolve intelligence gaps by requiring various programs, divisions, and personnel to work together to identify, gather, and assess information for intelligence.

EXHIBIT 9: THE FBI INTELLIGENCE CYCLE

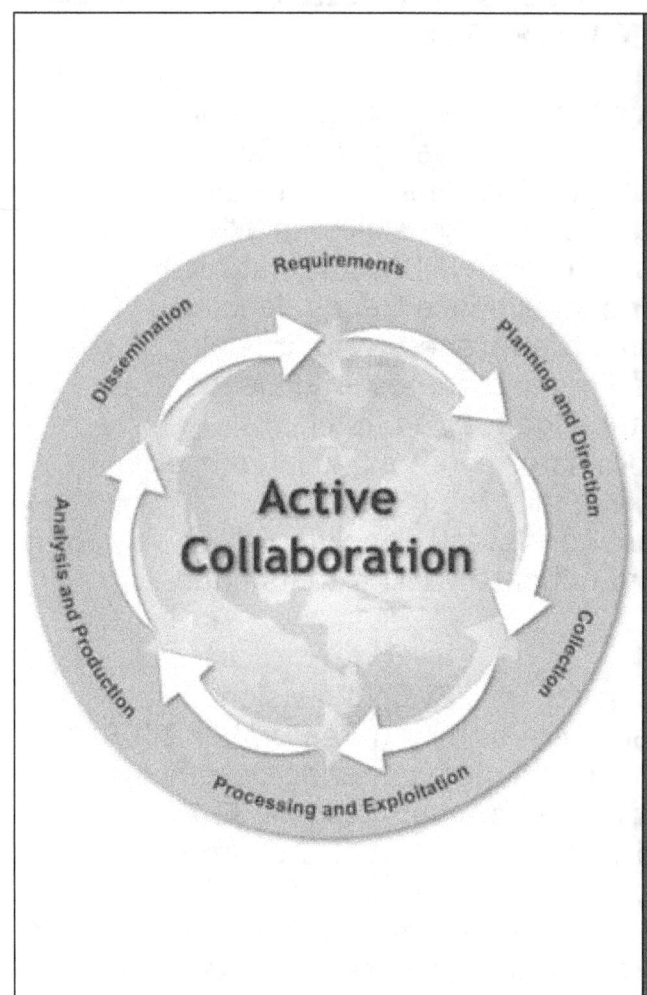

1. **Requirements**. Specific and most significant information needs, as established by the Director of National Intelligence and other U.S. Intelligence Agencies.

2. **Planning and Direction**. Managing the effort to satisfy national requirements and identify FBI specific requirements.

3. **Collection**. Gathering raw information through interviews, liaisons, surveillance, operations, and searches.

4. **Processing and Exploitation**. Decrypting, translating, and reducing information into a usable format for analysts.

5. **Analysis and Production**. Converting raw information into intelligence by evaluating its validity, placing it in context, drawing conclusions, and preparing raw or finished intelligence products.

6. **Dissemination**. Distributing raw or finished intelligence to the U.S. Intelligence Community in response to specific requirements.

Source: FBI Directorate of Intelligence

Within this intelligence cycle, collecting information is just one part of a larger effort that guides the constant processing, analysis, and dissemination of intelligence. The FBI uses this intelligence cycle to pinpoint specific instances of criminal or terrorist concern, such as suspicious chemical purchases or malicious threat letters. The resulting information, often fragmented and unrelated, is analyzed and paired with similar data trends that allow the FBI to identify national security gaps and vulnerabilities. To address identified gaps and vulnerabilities, the FBI relies on communication and information sharing between its programs to connect and shape new information with conventional intelligence. In addition to producing and disseminating intelligence reports, the FBI uses the information from this cycle to establish new intelligence collection requirements.

Various FBI groups, such as the Directorate of Intelligence, the WMD Directorate, and the Field Intelligence Group at each field division, identify and process WMD information in the intelligence cycle. These groups each have WMD intelligence responsibilities that transcend traditional intelligence and investigative roles.[18] The Directorate of Intelligence administers all intelligence activities at FBI headquarters and ensures that intelligence collection and analysis is conducted across the FBI's investigative programs through the Field Intelligence Groups.

Embedded within the WMD Directorate, the Directorate of Intelligence's Intelligence and Analysis Section (IAS) manages and supports WMD-specific investigations by targeting, identifying, and assessing counterterrorism and proliferation threats. Field Intelligence Groups at each field division work to identify, collect, and report raw and finished intelligence to the Directorate of Intelligence and other members of the U.S. Intelligence Community. Intelligence Analysts staff each Field Intelligence Group and work to identify trends, assess and evaluate potential threats, and aid field divisions in assembling fragmented intelligence information. Field division Intelligence Analysts also assist Special Agents in drafting, editing, and disseminating intelligence products to ensure that field division intelligence is accurate and developed according to intelligence reporting requirements.

Although the groups within the FBI's intelligence cycle have distinct roles and responsibilities, they have been organized to work together in their efforts to prevent WMD attacks. By sharing the capabilities of IAS, the WMD Directorate and the Directorate of Intelligence can help ensure that national investigative and intelligence activities are coordinated.

In addition to performing its traditional WMD casework responsibilities, the WMD Directorate and the WMD Coordinators have begun identifying and sharing WMD-specific intelligence with some Field Intelligence Groups. However, as shown by Exhibit 10, the method by which groups within the FBI's WMD program share and assess intelligence does not facilitate an active working relationship between field division Intelligence Analysts and WMD Coordinators. This lack of a standardized communication channel creates a risk that these field division units will not continuously exchange information on local WMD threats and vulnerabilities.

---

[18] As part of the FBI's ongoing initiative to realign its capacity to identify, assess, and report domestic intelligence, the Field Intelligence Groups and their Intelligence Analysts have begun applying their specialized intelligence skills to support specific investigative programs.

EXHIBIT 10: WMD PROGRAM INTELLIGENCE ORGANIZATION

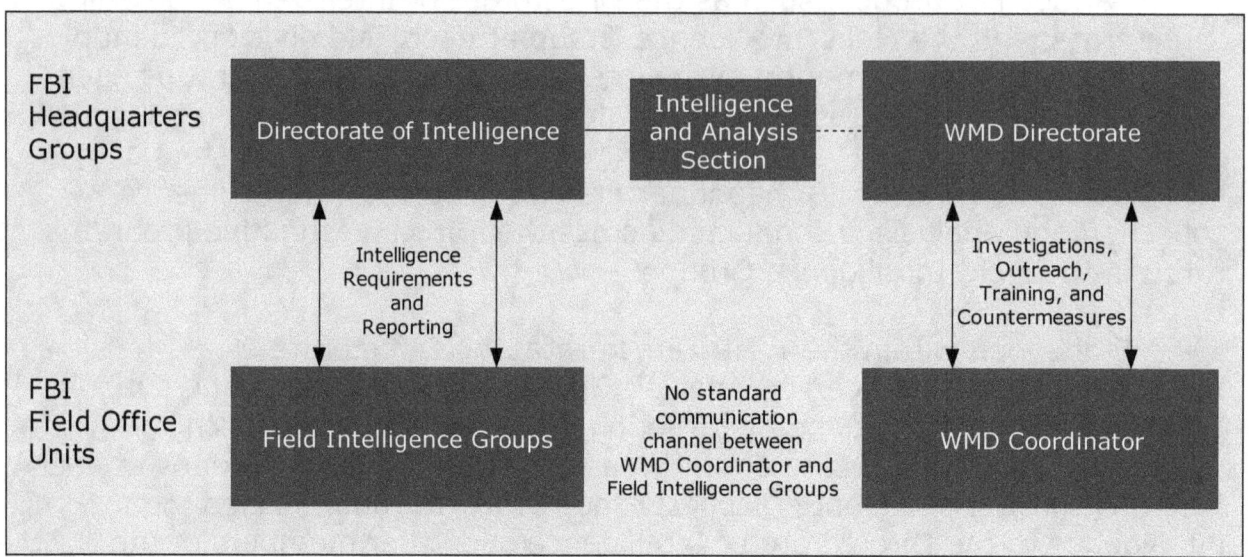

Source: OIG analysis of the Directorate of Intelligence and WMD Directorate

In view of the role of WMD Coordinators as WMD subject matter experts, we believe that the structure used to identify and assess WMD intelligence in the field divisions must involve the WMD Coordinator. WMD Coordinators need to efficiently acquire and effectively use WMD intelligence to address prioritized domain needs. Additionally, Intelligence Analysts need to be positioned to assist WMD Coordinators in accomplishing activities that address WMD domain threats and vulnerabilities.

The following section describes why the FBI's WMD intelligence framework should include a formal method by which WMD Coordinators and field division Intelligence Analysts can collaborate.

WMD Coordinator and Intelligence Analyst Collaboration

Most WMD Coordinators were appointed to their position from Special Agent investigative backgrounds, while Intelligence Analysts have specialized information assessment training that offers different perspectives on WMD matters. One WMD Directorate official said that unlike WMD Coordinators, "Intelligence Analysts are taught to fish" for threats in the WMD domain. Intelligence Analysts can gather information on intelligence trends for WMD Coordinators, suggest questions to pose during human source interviews, and provide best practices on how to fulfill the FBI's intelligence report requirements, mitigate threats, and prepare an adequate incident response through domain management. If the FBI ensured that WMD Coordinators and Intelligence Analysts work together, it would be better positioned to identify WMD threats and vulnerabilities to address domain needs.

As discussed in Finding I, the WMD Directorate is using Field Intelligence Group Intelligence Analysts to conduct WMD domain assessments for each field division without requiring that the information be shared with the WMD Coordinators. WMD Coordinators we interviewed provided several reasons why an enhanced intelligence sharing capability is necessary on a day-to-day basis for the WMD program. Besides the need for regular access to WMD intelligence, Coordinators also stated that Intelligence Analyst assistance would help them navigate the FBI and larger U.S. Intelligence Community's intelligence apparatus.

Need for Field Division WMD Intelligence Support

WMD Directorate officials told us that WMD Coordinators have not been satisfied with their access to Field Intelligence Group resources. WMD Coordinators have also stated that inconsistent coordination with field division Intelligence Analysts negatively affects their ability to identify and report WMD issues. Because of their responsibilities to teach WMD awareness and response, perform outreach, and institute effective countermeasures, some WMD Coordinators told us that they need assistance to identify threats, assess vulnerabilities, and draft intelligence reports. WMD Coordinators also told us that assistance from Intelligence Analysts would allow them to expand their WMD knowledge, extend their capacity to inform liaisons and perform outreach, and acquire the information necessary to produce accurate and useful intelligence reports.

According to FBI officials, designating specific Intelligence Analysts to work on counterproliferation investigations has led to successful program results. In December 2006, the WMD Directorate requested that each field division designate an Intelligence Analyst to support newly established Counterproliferation Coordinators on related casework.[19] This designation has provided Intelligence Analysts the opportunity to become specialized in counterproliferation trends and skills aimed at preventing and neutralizing efforts to obtain WMDs illegally. Although Intelligence Analysts under this model have been assigned to work with Special Agents on counterproliferation cases, they still report to Field Intelligence Group supervisors and day-to-day program activities are managed between the

---

[19] In FY 2007, the WMD Directorate established Counterproliferation Coordinators in each field division to work with the Counterintelligence and Counterterrorism Divisions to prevent or neutralize the trafficking of WMD and dual-use technologies. As the field division's contact for all counterproliferation investigations, the Counterproliferation Coordinator interacts with the WMD Coordinator.

Special Agents and Intelligence Analysts. One Intelligence Analyst conducting both WMD and counterproliferation intelligence duties told us that the WMD Directorate should issue similar guidance to promote greater collaboration between WMD Coordinators and Intelligence Analysts.

Status of Intelligence Analyst Collaboration with WMD Coordinators

The FBI does not typically require that a field division Intelligence Analyst work directly with the WMD Coordinator. WMD Directorate records indicate that as of January 2009 only 21 of 56 field divisions, or 38 percent, designated a specific Intelligence Analyst to work with the WMD Coordinator. Instead, field divisions generally assign analysts to work on WMD concerns based on the field division's priorities and resources. Some field divisions with a history of domestic terrorism incidents, such as Oklahoma City or New York, provided designated intelligence support to potential WMD investigations. Other field divisions also have their WMD Coordinators work closely with designated Intelligence Analysts. According to these field division managers and personnel, cooperation between WMD Coordinators and Intelligence Analysts has fostered greater knowledge of WMD domain entities.

In the Oklahoma City Field Division, for example, the designated Intelligence Analyst leverages the WMD Coordinator's outreach by constructing geospatial maps of key resources in the region, including agricultural facilities, water treatment plants, and oil pipelines, and by reaching out to interagency partners. In the New York Field Division, the Intelligence Analyst designated to work with the WMD Coordinator attends case and human source interviews. The Intelligence Analyst participates alongside the Coordinator by gathering testimonial information that addresses specific WMD intelligence requirements. The analyst also provides strategic intelligence support to on-going WMD cases. The value added to the division's WMD program from intelligence collaboration has also led the division to propose a WMD analysis group to support the WMD Coordinator's domain awareness.

In contrast, we found that many field divisions that have not experienced major terrorism events have dedicated Intelligence Analysts to other investigative programs such as violent or white-collar crimes and are not assigning the analysts any WMD intelligence duties. Some field divisions assigned Intelligence Analysts to support a specific program or squad, while others had Intelligence Analysts simultaneously identify, assess, and prepare intelligence for many different investigative programs.

We found one instance where WMD officials from a large field division requested help from field division Intelligence Analysts to develop and provide on-going analysis of key industry and infrastructure elements within the field division that could be linked to the production, use, or deployment of a WMD. In their request, WMD officials described their need of a designated Intelligence Analyst so that they could perform subsequent strategic reviews of these elements. However, the division's Field Intelligence Group leadership perceived the project as an extension of investigative casework. Leadership declined to assign an Intelligence Analyst and instead recommended that the WMD program perform this review by hiring a contractor. In contrast, another Field Intelligence Group proactively determined that it should evaluate its infrastructure as a foundation for greater domain awareness, and it designated an Intelligence Analyst to help develop, identify, and assess similar infrastructure entities within the field division.

Although field division intelligence officials said they did not object to supporting WMD initiatives, we found that some were reluctant to assign analysts to specific investigative programs, including WMD. Some of these officials told us that they believe Intelligence Analysts and Special Agents do not understand their respective responsibilities and approaches to accomplishing their work. Special Agents assigned to counterterrorism or WMD squads focus on activities that prepare for, respond to, and contain terrorist acts. Intelligence Analysts working on similar matters need to spend much of their time evaluating raw, fragmented data and using analytical tools to forecast potential threats facing the field division. As a result, an Intelligence Analyst may not always have the time to proactively support Special Agents with their case duties. Field Intelligence Group officials also stated that they are cognizant of the amount of administrative management that casework requires. These officials expressed concern that a close collaboration between Intelligence Analysts and Special Agents will lead to Special Agents assigning Intelligence Analysts unwanted administrative case duties, such as answering the telephone or making photocopies.

While we understand the concern of Field Intelligence Group officials that Intelligence Analysts may be used for administrative case functions, we believe that the FBI needs to find a method for ensuring the close collaboration of WMD Coordinators and Intelligence Analysts. As explained below, the FBI has instituted a new process for increasing collaboration between Special Agents and Intelligence Analysts. However, we have concerns about whether this process will ensure an adequate level of coordination between Intelligence Analysts and WMD Coordinators.

Ongoing Efforts to Designate Certain Intelligence Analyst Functions

The FBI has indicated that many field divisions lack direction about the type of intelligence that each Field Intelligence Group should obtain and analyze. To help address these issues, the FBI began reorganizing its field division intelligence operations through its Strategic Execution Team (SET). Comprised of nearly 100 agents, analysts, and other FBI professionals, SET has: (1) evaluated how an array of field divisions handled intelligence, (2) identified best practices to define an "optimal model for intelligence" for every field division, and (3) instituted these models across the FBI. In establishing each field division's optimal intelligence model, the FBI expects SET to refocus field operations to encourage all FBI personnel to support its intelligence efforts.

In December 2008, SET established a standard organizational model for Field Intelligence Groups to manage five core field division intelligence functions, as shown by Exhibit 11.[20] The FBI believes that these intelligence functions, managed by appointed Special Agents or Intelligence Analysts, will facilitate the exchange of information about specific domain entities across all field division programs.

---

[20] The FBI's standardized Field Intelligence Group structure provides specific functions and leadership positions to implement in each field division; however, it also accounts for variations in office size and composition. Therefore, the FBI developed three similar Field Intelligence Group models for application in small, medium, and large field divisions.

EXHIBIT 11: REALIGNED FIELD INTELLIGENCE GROUP FUNCTIONS

Function	Designated Intelligence Analyst(s) or Special Agent(s)	Responsibilities
Domain Management	Domain Management Coordinator	• Implement and operate a strategy that continuously identifies a field division's area of responsibility. • Produce domain assessments and publications. • Identify intelligence gaps and detect threat patterns.
Collection Management	Collection Management Coordinator	• Coordinate the field division's intelligence collection efforts. • Develop intelligence collection strategy and plan.
Requirements Collection	Special Agent Human Intelligence Collector	• Identify, assess, develop, and recruit human sources to address intelligence requirements. • Evaluate the authenticity, reliability, and control of sources. • Form liaisons to identify threats and acquire confidential sources.
Tactical Intelligence	Intelligence Analyst Embedded with Operational Squad	• Interpret intelligence collection requirements. • Assist with targeting projects to develop new sources. • Develop a local targeting strategy to identify new intelligence opportunities.
Intelligence Production & Dissemination	Chief Reports Officer	• Accountable for production of accurate, timely, and professional raw intelligence. • Reviews all raw intelligence to protect sources, validates methods and adds value.

Source: FBI SET New Field Intelligence handbook, Version 1.5

In August 2008, the FBI started providing field division Intelligence Analysts with extensive training at FBI headquarters to address specific expectations with regard to these new intelligence and management roles. The FBI anticipates that after initial training is completed in October 2009 the field divisions should be able to begin integrating a complete intelligence cycle that addresses key domain threats.

In conjunction with SET, WMD Coordinators told us that they have begun working in an informal capacity with their Field Intelligence Groups to identify and develop intelligence on WMD threats and vulnerabilities. However, WMD Coordinators, Intelligence Analysts, and SET program officials indicated that they do not know how specific SET functions and positions will interact and support WMD Coordinator work in obtaining and sharing WMD intelligence. Therefore, once SET is finalized, the potential still exists that some field divisions will not assign specific intelligence personnel to work with the WMD Coordinator.

SET's intelligence reorganization demonstrates that the FBI believes field division Intelligence Analysts can be designated specific roles. For example, Intelligence Analysts performing SET Tactical Intelligence functions will report to a field division tactical intelligence supervisor but serve on a field division investigative squad. These Intelligence Analysts will be required to assist the squad with real-time intelligence reporting, the interpretation and use of intelligence requirements, the identification and collection of intelligence, and the analysis of information derived from investigations.

We recommend that the FBI require that each field division designate an Intelligence Analyst to meet with the WMD Coordinator periodically and discuss their planned work and activities and provide feedback on whether these activities will address prioritized domain needs. In view of the WMD domain assessment initiative, which has assigned specific field division Intelligence Analysts to work with the WMD Directorate to prioritize threats and vulnerabilities facing each field division, we believe these Intelligence Analysts present the most appropriate Field Intelligence Group conduit for the WMD Coordinator. Such a designation would also allow these Intelligence Analysts to refine their WMD knowledge and skills and therefore enhance WMD intelligence capabilities at each field division.

Regarding the concerns of Field Intelligence Group officials about how designated Intelligence Analysts would be used to assist investigative aspects of the WMD program, we believe that the FBI needs to ensure that designated Intelligence Analysts are used appropriately to identify, assess, and report WMD intelligence instead of being assigned to work on ancillary case duties.

Enhancing FBI WMD Intelligence Reporting Capability

Intelligence report dissemination is critical to the FBI's WMD program because it is the primary means for communicating WMD threats and vulnerabilities throughout the FBI and larger U.S. Intelligence Community. It is also critical for identifying, addressing, and developing new intelligence requirements to enhance the field division's WMD domain awareness and influence U.S. national security policy. The FBI communicates WMD intelligence between its programs and to other intelligence agencies mainly through three types of intelligence products, shown in Exhibit 12.

EXHIBIT 12: EXAMPLES OF FBI INTELLIGENCE REPORT PRODUCTS

Report Format	Information Type
Intelligence Information Report	Reports raw, unevaluated, and new data using established intelligence standards.
Intelligence Assessment	Evaluates data that identifies specific threats or trends.
Intelligence Bulletin	Assesses significant criminal or national security developments and may not contain recommendations.

Source: FBI Directorate of Intelligence

Because intelligence production is such a significant part of the WMD Coordinator's knowledge of WMD threats and vulnerabilities, we reviewed the types and quantity of WMD intelligence produced by field divisions. We found that WMD Coordinators who worked closely with designated Intelligence Analysts were able to enhance their knowledge and expertise. They expanded their knowledge of ongoing WMD intelligence trends, field division analytical infrastructure studies, and familiarity with the FBI's intelligence cycle and requirements. We believe that this type of working relationship should be promoted between all Intelligence Analysts and WMD Coordinators in order to enhance the skills of WMD Coordinators and increase the number of well-sourced WMD intelligence reports.

Intelligence Reporting Requirements

Field division Intelligence Analysts may write intelligence reports themselves or assist Special Agents, including WMD Coordinators, in developing and writing intelligence reports. However, intelligence requirements related to chemical, biological, radiological, or nuclear terrorism, promulgated by both Directorate of Intelligence and the larger U.S. Intelligence Community, govern how to collect, produce, and disseminate intelligence. These WMD requirements instruct analysts to report specific information such as attempts to procure specific chemicals, agents, or dispersal devices, or finite environmental signs of a WMD incident. The requirements also include specified intelligence formats and timeframes. In addition, U.S. Intelligence Community reporting standards also influence how the FBI should format its intelligence reports.

Intelligence reporting requirements and standards require that the FBI devote specific units to develop draft intelligence reports, check drafted reports against reporting standards, and disseminate approved reports to the broader U.S. Intelligence Community. The WMD Directorate works with the Directorate of Intelligence's Reports Section to draft intelligence reports that comply with both FBI requirements and non-FBI requirements. Reporting requirements can be adjusted if information pertains to an imminent chemical, biological, radiological, or nuclear threat or addresses a new but not previously identified intelligence need. However, Field Intelligence Groups do not normally disseminate WMD intelligence reports on their own. Instead, they work with the FBI's Directorate of Intelligence and the WMD Directorate to release intelligence reports to other members of the U.S. Intelligence Community.[21]

Field Division Intelligence Report Production

To gain a greater perspective on the volume of WMD intelligence drafted by FBI field divisions, we reviewed the number of intelligence reports issued by field division as detailed in the FBI field division June 2008 Semi-Annual Program Review.[22] The Semi-Annual Program Review period covered activity between October 2007 and June 2008. We found that 30 field divisions, or more than half of all FBI field divisions, did not finalize and disseminate a single WMD intelligence product. Meanwhile, only nine field divisions disseminated five or more WMD intelligence products. As shown in Exhibit 13, four field divisions disseminated two-thirds of the field division WMD intelligence products.[23]

---

[21] The FBI believes that if field divisions directly disseminate intelligence to the U.S. Intelligence Community, it can improve the timeliness of intelligence products. In designating a Chief Reports Officer at each field division, the FBI hopes to ensure that field division generated intelligence adheres to requirements and quality standards. However, limited technology and the need for FBI headquarters to approve sensitive interagency, legal, and human source information has prevented field divisions from directly disseminating WMD intelligence products. Appendix III provides additional details regarding the process the FBI uses to review and disseminate WMD intelligence reports.

[22] In evaluating the number of WMD intelligence reports disseminated by FBI field divisions, we encountered several variables in the data available to us that led us to rely on intelligence statistics reported in individual field division Semi-Annual Program Review results. These variables included: (1) inconsistent data availability timeframes because the FBI did not start to subcategorize WMD intelligence from counterterrorism intelligence until April 2008, and (2) various reconciliation issues between FBI system intelligence statistics and statistics reported by WMD Coordinators in field division Semi-Annual Program Reviews.

[23] The number of WMD intelligence reports produced by field divisions does not necessarily correlate to superior investigative or intelligence activity of those field divisions. However, the number of reports issued was the only metric available that allowed us to compare intelligence reporting capacity between field divisions and assess the overall ability of each to identify and collect WMD intelligence.

EXHIBIT 13: FIELD DIVISIONS DISSEMINATING THE MOST WMD INTELLIGENCE REPORTS BETWEEN OCTOBER 2007 AND JUNE 2008

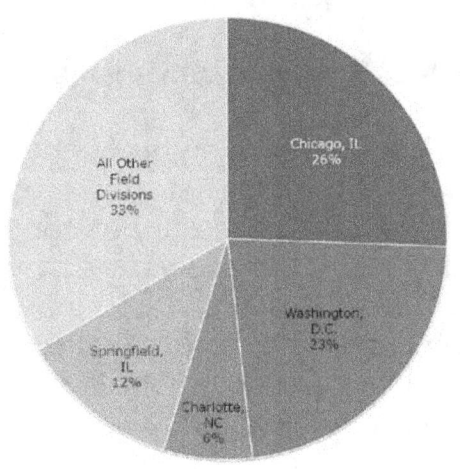

Field Division	Number of WMD Intelligence Reports
Chicago, IL	43
Washington, D.C.	38
Charlotte, NC	11
Springfield, IL	20
All Other Field Divisions	56
TOTAL	**168**

Source: OIG Analysis of FY 2008 FBI Semi-Annual Program Review
Note: Percentages in pie chart rounded to total 100 percent.

We found that field divisions able to disseminate the largest number of WMD intelligence reports had an established approach or process in how they handled their intelligence reporting.

Although our review did not find that designated WMD Intelligence Analysts necessarily increased the overall intelligence production of the field division, WMD Coordinators told us that a more structured intelligence apparatus would help them identify and report WMD intelligence. For example, Coordinators cited instances where, without Intelligence Analyst support, they submitted draft intelligence reports for Directorate of Intelligence approval but the intelligence reports were sent back because the reports did not: (1) consistently meet intelligence requirements, (2) adhere to formatting standards, or (3) contain new or actionable information. As a result, the Directorate of Intelligence could not finalize and disseminate these WMD Coordinator-submitted draft reports. Directorate of Intelligence officials confirmed that the majority of intelligence reports are returned to field divisions for these reasons.

An official with the Directorate of Intelligence also confirmed that many Special Agents do not understand intelligence reporting requirements. As a result, Special Agents are often not successful at drafting intelligence that is complete, accurate, and correctly formatted for dissemination to other intelligence agencies. Some WMD Coordinators told us that their lack of intelligence reporting expertise has discouraged them from drafting additional intelligence products. However, since Intelligence Analysts serve as the field division experts in intelligence reporting, if WMD Coordinators worked more closely with them on WMD matters, Intelligence Analysts would be better positioned to assist WMD Coordinators in producing WMD intelligence reports that meet the standards for dissemination.

Supporting WMD Intelligence Analyst WMD Program Activities

Although Intelligence Analysts receive funding for analytical activities from their Field Intelligence Group, some analysts told us that they often lacked the field division and WMD Directorate support necessary to conduct additional analysis work on specific WMD activities. One analyst we interviewed noted an inability to acquire even basic WMD research materials. This Intelligence Analyst contacted the WMD Directorate for assistance, but was informed that the WMD Directorate could not purchase materials for this analyst because it does not "own" field division Intelligence Analysts, even if they contribute to WMD intelligence efforts.

We discussed the allocation of WMD-specific resources to finance Intelligence Analyst activities and research material with WMD Coordinators. Each fiscal year, WMD Coordinators submit a budget and receive, on average, an allocation of $15,000 from the WMD Directorate to support their investigative, outreach, and training activities. WMD Coordinators expressed a willingness to use these funds to help support analyst WMD activities. However, WMD Coordinators frequently mentioned that they were unaware that analysts required WMD materials such as manuals, handbooks, or analysis tools. One Coordinator with designated Field Intelligence Group support allocated funds for their analyst to attend WMD-specific training to enhance their WMD competency. Some WMD Coordinators stated that they used their budget allowances to support Special Agents working on other programs episodically, including hazardous materials and bomb response squads, because their work also supported WMD awareness and prevention.

In light of the FBI's efforts to restructure its WMD intelligence capabilities, the FBI should consider adjusting its strict programmatic budgetary approach to allow one program's resources to support another's, which would allow funds to support both investigative and analytical activities that together are part of a comprehensive WMD program.[24] As WMD Coordinators increasingly utilize Intelligence Analysts to identify and prioritize WMD threats and vulnerabilities, they will require a means to provide specific WMD analytical resources and training. The practice of

---

[24] The WMD Directorate allocates direct funds to WMD Coordinators to support WMD countermeasure, outreach, and training efforts in their field division. While field division WMD efforts receive lateral assistance from other squads and teams, Special Agents and Intelligence Analysts assisting the Coordinator request and receive direct funds from their designated FBI division, program, or unit.

separating Field Intelligence Groups and WMD budgets may become burdensome to field divisions trying to establish WMD expertise across intelligence and operational divisions.

Once field divisions designate Intelligence Analysts to work with a WMD Coordinator, we believe that the FBI has a responsibility to help ensure that these analysts have the tools necessary to effectively contribute to field division WMD efforts and the FBI's overall WMD prevention strategy. Therefore, we recommend that the FBI permit WMD Coordinators to consider purchases requested by designated WMD Intelligence Analysts in formulating their field division WMD budget requests.

Conclusion

WMD Coordinators face significant challenges in addressing prioritized WMD threats and vulnerabilities. It is therefore critical that the WMD Coordinators share information with Intelligence Analysts quickly. Although the FBI has established an organizational framework and comprehensive intelligence cycle in an effort to promote regular communication between programs, no formalized method facilitates collaboration between WMD Coordinators and designated Intelligence Analysts. As a result, we found limited WMD Coordinator interaction with Field Intelligence Groups relating to WMD threats and vulnerabilities. WMD Coordinators reported that the lack of analytical coordination on WMD matters with designated Intelligence Analysts has hindered them from fully acquiring intelligence necessary to identify specific WMD threats facing their field division.

Ongoing work between WMD Coordinators and Intelligence Analysts in some field divisions has resulted in useful infrastructure assessments and strategic intelligence reporting, which has increased the WMD Coordinators' awareness and management of their domains. WMD Coordinators who worked closely with at least one Intelligence Analyst, such as WMD Coordinators in the New York and Oklahoma City field divisions, said that their collaborative work resulted in increased familiarity with intelligence research methods and trends. Yet, varying field division priorities and a general reluctance to dedicate analytical capabilities to the WMD Coordinator program have resulted in only periodic interactions in other field divisions.

Intelligence analysis is a specialized role best facilitated by Intelligence Analysts. For the FBI to operate a continuous intelligence cycle that provides an ongoing flow of WMD intelligence, close and dedicated interaction between WMD Coordinators and Intelligence Analysts is essential. At the same time, WMD Coordinators must also recognize that they need to adequately fund and appropriately use designated intelligence support.

WMD Coordinators and analysts should work together to understand one another's capabilities and mission. Therefore, despite Field Intelligence Group officials' sentiments that Intelligence Analysts will be left to perform ancillary case duties when assigned to Special Agents, we believe that active coordination between these personnel can improve actionable WMD intelligence reporting that WMD Coordinators require to address their domain needs.

Recommendations

We recommend that the FBI:

7.   Require that each field division designate an Intelligence Analyst to meet with the WMD Coordinator periodically and discuss their planned work and activities and provide feedback on whether these activities will address prioritized domain needs.

8.   Permit WMD Coordinators to consider purchases requested by designated WMD Intelligence Analysts in formulating their field division WMD budget requests.

III. THE FBI NEEDS TO ENSURE WMD COORDINATORS AND INTELLIGENCE ANALYSTS CAN ADDRESS WMD DOMAIN NEEDS

Although the FBI relies on WMD Coordinators to detect and prevent WMDs at the field division level, the FBI has not established initial qualifications or required skills for these Coordinators. The FBI also has not provided formalized training plans to ensure that WMD Coordinators and Intelligence Analysts develop the skills necessary to achieve comprehensive WMD domain awareness. Further, the FBI identified the lack of a systemic methodology or comprehensive ability to accurately track training that its WMD personnel have received. Without training requirements and tracking capabilities, the FBI cannot identify gaps in skills, reprioritize resources to mitigate those gaps, and ensure WMD preparedness throughout the FBI.

The WMD Directorate is responsible for identifying, developing, and offering WMD training throughout the FBI. Since its inception in 2006, the WMD Directorate has substantially increased the number of training courses and exercises offered to WMD Coordinators, other FBI Special Agents and Intelligence Analysts, and law enforcement personnel at federal, state, and local agencies. During FY 2006, the WMD Directorate hosted and participated in 16 training exercises and provided instruction to 1,200 participants. Just 2 years later, in FY 2008, the WMD Directorate hosted and participated in over 90 exercises that provided WMD training to almost 7,000 people in law enforcement and private industries. The Directorate has also expanded the type of training subjects it hosts or helps host to ensure that training is offered in each major WMD area – chemical, biological, radiological, and nuclear.

WMD Coordinators are responsible for training other FBI Special Agents and field division personnel about detecting, handling, and responding to WMDs. Because they serve as their field division's WMD subject matter expert and need to conduct activities to address domain needs, WMD Coordinators require specialized training on the highly technical and advanced nature of the WMD threats and vulnerabilities that may be present in their respective WMD domain. Senior WMD Directorate officials explained to us that different types of WMDs require specialized training because the efforts needed to detect, mitigate, and handle chemical, biological, radiological, and nuclear materials vary considerably.

The following section discusses how the FBI identifies WMD training needs and determines whether it has adequately prepared its WMD Coordinators to address their specific WMD domain needs. In addition,

47

because effective WMD domain management requires that WMD Coordinators and Intelligence Analysts work together to prioritize and address WMD threats and vulnerabilities, this section also assesses the WMD training courses offered to FBI Intelligence Analysts who work with WMD Coordinators.

Lack of Written WMD Coordinator Qualifications

The WMD Directorate does not usually select specific Special Agents to be WMD Coordinators. Instead, field divisions are responsible for determining who should be WMD Coordinators. Even though WMD Coordinators are not selected or approved by the WMD Directorate, the FBI recognizes the specialized nature of their function and has designated the position as a "specialty-transfer" position at the field division level. This means that any Special Agent who receives WMD Coordinator training, even if they are not currently a WMD Coordinator, can transfer to another field division that needs a WMD Coordinator. Although WMD Coordinators require specialized training, the FBI has not provided field divisions with specific qualifications for the knowledge, skills, and abilities that WMD Coordinators require. However, designated field division positions similar to the WMD Coordinator have written qualifications and required skill sets that detail specific skills and abilities for the position. For example, field division management uses a list of required skill sets to help assess whether an applicant has the skills necessary to serve successfully as a Counterproliferation Coordinator.[25]

The lack of written qualifications for the WMD Coordinator position has affected the WMD program in at least two ways. Without knowing the specific skills and abilities required by the position, field division supervisors may not select the most qualified Special Agents as WMD Coordinators. Moreover, without written qualifications, already designated WMD Coordinators may not know what additional training or skills they need to acquire to be an effective WMD Coordinator. By providing field divisions with WMD Coordinator qualifications, the FBI would allow field divisions to either identify agents that can immediately begin conducting WMD outreach, training, and countermeasures or to identify what training should be provided to those agents who lack the qualifications to immediately step into the WMD Coordinator position. Therefore, we recommend that the FBI develop and disseminate WMD Coordinator position qualifications to field

---

[25] The field division's Counterproliferation Coordinator is responsible for coordinating all Counterproliferation investigative programs and conducting liaison with the U.S. Attorneys Office, and other intelligence and law enforcement agencies working proliferation matters. Counterproliferation Coordinators also assist Counterproliferation Analysts in identifying counterproliferation issues for dissemination to FBI and outside entities.

division management and current WMD Coordinators to use in appointing future WMD Coordinators and for delineating the necessary skills and abilities current WMD Coordinators should obtain.

Identifying and Tracking WMD Training Requirements and Gaps

FBI policies require that the WMD Directorate track and report the WMD training obtained by its personnel. However, we found that the WMD Directorate lacked the mechanisms necessary to track and report WMD training accurately and as a result, could not easily ascertain whether WMD Coordinator and Intelligence Analysts received adequate training.

Assessment of Preliminary WMD Training Tracking Activity

The FBI's Virtual Academy is the official online-based training system that the FBI uses to track personnel training.[26] The system, developed and operated by the FBI's Virtual Academy Unit, provides FBI personnel a means to access their official training records, register for FBI courses, and track portions of their own training. However, as of October 2008, the Virtual Academy system could not track any non-FBI training, including field training exercises, tabletop exercises, international training, or other federal, state, or local training.[27] Because the FBI does not provide the vast majority of available WMD-related training and Virtual Academy did not record training offered by other agencies and groups, field divisions have been left to track WMD training locally either on paper or by using electronic spreadsheets.

As of October 2008, the WMD Directorate had only one method readily available to track WMD training received by WMD Coordinators: the statistical accomplishment report. However, the WMD Directorate has not been capturing and consolidating information provided on the statistical accomplishment activity reports in a way that allows it to assess the training needs of its field division WMD personnel. Since the WMD Directorate has not been using activity reports to track WMD training, it cannot readily

---

[26] As an internal learning management system, Virtual Academy was not intended to track non-FBI training. Instead, the FBI established Virtual Academy to serve as a structured, efficient, and electronically delivered learning system for FBI personnel, pertinent forensic scientists, and other law enforcement officers.

[27] During our audit, the FBI began working on a new Virtual Academy module that will allow personnel to upload and track information pertaining to non-FBI coursework. However, because these enhancements were not implemented during our audit, we could not test them to determine if they provide FBI officials the ability to track WMD training and identify field division personnel WMD knowledge gaps.

assess whether the field division has the knowledge, skills, and abilities to detect or handle WMDs.

Training Readiness Management System

Because FBI employees receive non-FBI WMD training that cannot be tracked by Virtual Academy, the WMD Directorate could not use Virtual Academy to ascertain the WMD training readiness of each field division. Consequently, in September 2008 the WMD Directorate issued a Statement of Work to have a contractor begin expanding and developing new modules to another database called the Training Readiness Management System (Management System). Originally used to track the FBI Hostage Rescue Team and Critical Incident Response Group training and readiness, the Management System required significant modifications to meet new WMD Directorate tracking and training information requirements. Because these modifications are still being made and additional testing needs to be performed, FBI officials said they have not set an expected date for completing the Management System.

The Management System will have eight modules and provide the WMD Directorate the ability to access training records and capture WMD readiness training levels across different field divisions.[28] In addition, Management System planning documents indicate that it will have the capability to enable the FBI to reprioritize training and other resources based on new and emerging WMD threats and vulnerabilities and track and report training and readiness information, as shown by Exhibit 14.

---

[28] The modules within the Training Management Readiness System consist of the following: (1) Individual Training, (2) Collective Training, (3) Individual Readiness and Collective Readiness Levels, (4) Equipment, (5) Training Management, (6) Personnel Management, (7) Resource Management, and (8) Risk Management.

EXHIBIT 14: SELECTED TRAINING READINESS MANAGEMENT SYSTEM FEATURES[29]

Administrative Features	• Contains WMD Directorate standard operating procedures, lesson plans, and training curriculum. • Navigates through the training approval screen that maps to designated training. • Incorporates screening criteria for approval authority based on task.
Accessibility Features	• Enables WMD Directorate leaders, staff, and personnel to view training, readiness, equipment, references, and education resources • Designated leaders and managers can view training calendars and exercises. • Leaders at all levels can access their respective unit's status in terms of training and mission essential and nonessential task lists.
Tracking, Assessing, and Reporting Features	• "Exercise (or Training) Status Page" – includes a feature that highlights events that have passed, not been evaluated, or deferred. • Manages individual initial qualifications and recurring certifications. • Empirical assessments of organizational preparedness, multi-layered operational proficiency, staff and support personnel proficiency. • Provides for automated after action reviews and self-assessment. • Incorporates pre-determined reports based on WMD Directorate input (e.g. unit task readiness, trends, user permissions, task periodicities and weightings, current report formats). • Tracks costs associated with training based on user inputs. • Produces status reports as specified by the user.
Prioritization Features	• Provides for management and prioritization of training exercises, events, and resources. • Enables reprioritization of training based on new missions or emerging threats.
Integration Features	• Provides for integration of training with operations.

Source: OIG overview of Training Readiness Management System features

---

[29] The elements detailed by Exhibit 14 have been categorized by the OIG based on our interpretation of the feature and are those we deemed most necessary to access, assess, and track WMD training accurately so that the WMD Directorate can identify gaps and reprioritize resources as necessary to ascertain and increase WMD readiness.

Once the FBI and its contractor update the Management System, the WMD Directorate will have administrator access to the system, although field division personnel will not. Instead, WMD Coordinators, Intelligence Analysts, and JTTF members who receive WMD training will need to use new Virtual Academy modules to upload their training information. Because field division personnel will not be able to directly enter training data in the Management System, the WMD Directorate will have to export Virtual Academy training records to the Management System on a regular basis.

WMD Directorate officials told us that through these Management System modules, they will be able to track WMD training of both internal Special Agents acting as WMD Coordinators and Intelligence Analysts as well as external law enforcement partners and JTTF members. This system should also allow the Directorate to identify gaps and increase and capture WMD readiness. These additional capabilities should allow the WMD Directorate to reprioritize resources and training where it's most needed.

However, the Management System will not interface with Virtual Academy, which has served as the FBI's official tracking system for training. Although we recognize the importance of the reporting and analysis benefits the Management System will provide to the WMD Directorate, the FBI should have a method to regularly reconcile Management System data with Virtual Academy data to ensure that both systems' training information is accurate and complete. Furthermore, regular reconciliation will enhance the reliability of the data used by the WMD Directorate to ascertain the WMD readiness of field division personnel. Therefore, we recommend that the FBI develop and implement a method that shares and reconciles Training Readiness Management System data with Virtual Academy records.

WMD Coordinator Training Initiatives

We interviewed WMD Coordinators at several field divisions and noted that they generally had different backgrounds, experience, training, and education levels. While all WMD Coordinators received standard Special Agent training at the FBI Academy in Quantico, Virginia, many had not received specialized WMD training before they were designated as their field division's WMD Coordinator. To ensure that WMD Coordinators have the skills and abilities they need to serve as their field division's WMD subject matter expert, the WMD Directorate has been developing additional WMD training opportunities for these personnel. As of October 2008, the WMD Directorate has been working on two major WMD Coordinator training initiatives. First, the WMD Directorate has begun developing a certification program that will serve as a training plan for WMD Coordinators. Second, the WMD Directorate has partnered with a higher educational institution to offer an advanced degree WMD training program for WMD Coordinators and other interested WMD personnel.

WMD Certification Program

In FY 2006, the WMD Directorate began developing a WMD certification program for all WMD Coordinators which will serve as a training plan to guide WMD Coordinator development and learning. According to Directorate officials, the certification program will include "hands on" training on specific WMD areas. In addition, portions of the draft certification program include rotational threat-based training that WMD Coordinators will need to complete every 18 months.

However, the WMD certification program has encountered some developmental issues that have prevented it from being finalized. For example, the WMD Directorate reported that it has had difficulty deciding whether current WMD Coordinators, including those who have served in the position for many years, must be required to attend the same training courses as newly designated or less experienced WMD Coordinators. In addition, because WMD Coordinators have different WMD skills and abilities, the WMD Directorate has had trouble deciding how the certification program should be tailored to individual WMD Coordinators. Because it has not yet resolved all of these issues, the FBI has not been able to finalize the WMD certification program and to date there are no official training requirements or training plan for WMD Coordinators or other personnel working with WMDs.

We believe that a certification program that aligns training needs with domain priorities would help improve the WMD Coordinators' skills and help in their performance of domain-related activities. WMD Directorate officials stated that they are "on track" to instituting their certification program for WMD Coordinators by the end of FY 2009. We recommend the FBI: (1) finalize its WMD Coordinator certification program opportunities, and (2) ensure that the finalized certification program offers threat-based courses based on the WMD domain threats and vulnerabilities within a WMD Coordinator's field division.

Continuing Higher Education Program

In 2008, the WMD Directorate began a continuing higher education program, referred to as the masters program, with the Indiana University of Pennsylvania to enhance WMD training for Special Agents and Intelligence Analysts. The program offers participants up to 30 academic credits. The initial 15 credits, referred to as the WMD Masters Certificate of Recognition Program (Phase 1), will be incorporated as part of the FBI's certification program. Phase 1 includes five courses designed to provide FBI WMD personnel with additional training in criminology, hazardous materials, and disaster preparedness.[30] After Phase 1, participants have the option to acquire 15 more credits via the program's second phase, referred to as the Master's Degree Completion Program (Phase 2). Phase 2 builds on the coursework offered by Phase 1 and focuses on quantitative WMD strategies, analysis, and research methods. While most of the available courses are part of the University's Masters in Criminology Program, almost all courses that are included in the curriculum for FBI personnel include a specific emphasis on the material most relevant to the FBI's role in WMD.

The masters program began in September 2008 with 18 WMD personnel from the FBI participating. The masters program continued with a second class that began on February 23, 2009, with 22 participants. As a result, 40 FBI personnel with a role in preventing WMD are on track to complete the Certificate of Recognition program in 2009. Further, 18 WMD personnel are enrolled in Phase 2 of the program and set to complete it by December 2009. As of February 2009 the FBI had spent $327,000 on all tuition costs, per diem, and other travel costs incurred by FBI employees attending these classes. While maintaining their full-time duties as FBI employees, program participants will attend lectures and seminars at the university, national laboratories, and FBI locations; and they must complete projects at the end of each program phase.

Due to the infancy of the masters program and the constantly changing nature of the risks and vulnerabilities surrounding WMD, the FBI should ensure that the course material included in the masters program continues to focus on the most relevant or pressing WMD concerns faced by WMD Coordinators and others working in the field divisions. Therefore, we recommend that the FBI implement a procedure by which the courses offered by the Indiana University of Pennsylvania Masters Certificate Program and Masters Degree Completion Program are regularly reviewed

---

[30] Appendix IV contains a list of continuing higher education program courses and their descriptions.

and assessed to ensure that course material address the changing needs of WMD Coordinators and Intelligence Analysts.

WMD Intelligence Analyst Training Efforts

The FBI has not established required skills or training requirements for Intelligence Analysts who work closely with WMD Coordinators and perform the WMD domain assessment.[31] Intelligence Analysts who worked on WMD matters exhibited a wide variety of backgrounds and have received training on general intelligence matters and requirements. To facilitate WMD Coordinator efforts to detect and prevent WMDs, Intelligence Analysts need to understand biological, chemical, nuclear, and radiological materials as they relate to or can be used as WMDs.

The FBI has offered general WMD training sessions for Intelligence Analysts and a 3-day WMD Analytical Conference sponsored by the WMD Directorate's embedded Intelligence and Analysis Section. According to WMD Directorate records, 83 percent of Intelligence Analysts who worked on WMD activities attended the WMD analytical conference. The conference consisted of internal FBI and external presentations, as well as threat briefings and exercises and was intended to educate analysts about WMD and foster the development of a larger WMD analytical community. In addition, the conference helped brief analysts on the basics of the WMD Directorate and its WMD program. The conference included practical exercises and case studies, including a WMD presentation from Department of Defense and presentations on counterproliferation, international, and domestic terrorism threats.

In spite of the course and conference offerings, Intelligence Analysts who worked with WMD Coordinators told us that they did not have a strong background in WMD or proficient knowledge of WMD related materials. We reviewed FBI Intelligence Analyst training records and found that many attended classes that provided overviews of WMD concerns such as a domestic terrorism class and a WMD Intelligence Analyst conference. However, we found that although the FBI has provided most of its Intelligence Analysts with a basic overview of WMD threats and vulnerabilities, many FBI Intelligence Analysts have either not received or have not recorded training on specific WMD areas, indicators, precursors, or trigger points.

---

[31] As discussed in Finding II, the Intelligence Analysts are coordinated by the FBI's Directorate of Intelligence, which establishes specific Intelligence Analyst training requirements.

Training Plans for WMD Intelligence Analysts

The FBI has not developed a WMD training plan for Intelligence Analysts who support the WMD Coordinators in domain management efforts. Some Intelligence Analysts told us that until July 2008 they had not received any guidance on what WMD courses they should take.[32] Instead, an official with the Directorate of Intelligence told us that the FBI sends WMD Intelligence Analysts to training outside the FBI for domain or specific types of intelligence training. For example, the WMD Directorate dispatches some Intelligence Analysts to courses held at the Central Intelligence Agency (CIA) due in part to its expanded WMD course options.

We compared the approach the FBI has used to train its WMD Intelligence Analysts to the method the Central Intelligence Agency uses to train its analysts. Unlike FBI Intelligence Analysts who have only been provided limited WMD training, CIA officials told us that their analysts must complete specialized courses before beginning work in a certain field. Furthermore, CIA analysts work closely with their supervisors to regularly identify and attend mission related intelligence courses. Additionally, the CIA also routinely offers its Intelligence Analysts training in a wide variety of WMD disciplines and modalities. According to CIA officials, the supervisory involvement in course selection, coupled with the availability of different course opportunities, reportedly allow these Intelligence Analysts to remain current on the changing threats and challenges facing the CIA.

Recognizing that Intelligence Analysts that work with WMD Coordinators need special skills and abilities, we recommend that the FBI develop a targeted WMD training plan encompassing both general and specific WMD-knowledge requirements for Intelligence Analysts who work with WMD Coordinators. Similar to our overall concerns regarding WMD Coordinator training, the finalized training plan should allow Intelligence Analysts to select training that addresses specific vulnerabilities and threats encompassed by their field division's WMD domain.

---

[32] The Directorate circulated an informal list of WMD classes in July 2008 to Intelligence Analysts – but only to analysts who had attended previous WMD Intelligence Analyst conferences. At that time the WMD Directorate issued a data call to various Intelligence Analysts that listed a series of classes, and asked them a series of questions including whether they believed the classes would help them compile intelligence reports and how long they had worked on WMD-related topics.

Conclusion

The FBI has not yet defined the qualifications and experience that WMD Coordinators require to achieve WMD subject matter expertise. Some field divisions have assigned Special Agents with limited to no prior WMD knowledge or skills to be WMD Coordinators. We recommend that the FBI identify the skills and abilities they need to become WMD subject matter experts.

To fully implement and sustain the WMD domain management process, WMD Coordinators and Intelligence Analysts need to receive specialized WMD threat-driven training. Although the WMD Directorate has developed and provided many training opportunities for its Coordinators, it has not defined a specialized training plan for them to use. Without such a required set of skills, background, or comprehensive training plan, the potential increases that WMD Coordinators and Intelligence Analysts will not be able to identify their domain threats and vulnerabilities. Because comprehensive domain knowledge relies on the integration of intelligence, we therefore believe it is important that both WMD Coordinators and any designated Intelligence Analysts receive training on specific WMD issues facing their field division. However, the FBI has not yet required that WMD Coordinators or Intelligence Analysts receive training that addresses the specific identified threats or vulnerabilities prioritized by field division domain assessments.

Moreover, the WMD Directorate is unable to access, track, and report accurately the training its WMD Coordinators, Intelligence Analysts, and other WMD personnel have received. Because of this, the Directorate cannot identify and assess WMD knowledge gaps and cannot effectively reprioritize resources to ensure that its personnel can adequately detect and prevent WMD attacks. Recognizing this deficiency, the WMD Directorate has begun to have the Training Readiness Management System customized to meet additional tracking and reporting requirements. Although this system will allow the Directorate to assess gaps in training, prioritize resources to mitigate those gaps, and also reprioritize training based on new and emerging WMD threats and vulnerabilities, it will not interface or communicate with Virtual Academy, which is the FBI's official training record. Because multiple training records increases the potential for inaccurate or incomplete reporting, the FBI needs to implement a means by which information in the Training Readiness Management System and Virtual Academy is regularly updated and reconciled.

Finally, the FBI has not developed training plans for the Intelligence Analysts that work on WMD investigations and collect WMD intelligence. Without ensuring that Intelligence Analysts acquire and maintain strong WMD knowledge and skills, the FBI cannot ensure that they will be able to identify WMD threats and vulnerabilities within their domain.

Recommendations

We recommend that the FBI:

9.   Develop and disseminate WMD Coordinator position qualifications to field division management and WMD Coordinators to use in appointing future WMD Coordinators and for delineating the necessary skills and abilities current WMD Coordinators should obtain.

10.   Develop and implement a method that shares and reconciles Training Readiness Management System data with Virtual Academy records.

11.   Finalize its WMD Coordinator certification program opportunities and ensure that the finalized certification program offers threat-based courses based on the WMD domain threats and vulnerabilities within a WMD Coordinator's field division.

12.   Implement a procedure by which the courses offered by the Indiana University of Pennsylvania Masters Certificate Program and Masters Degree Completion Program are regularly reviewed and assessed to ensure that course material address the changing needs of WMD Coordinators and Intelligence Analysts.

13.   Develop a targeted WMD training plan encompassing both general and specific WMD-knowledge requirements for Intelligence Analysts who work with WMD Coordinators that address the specific vulnerabilities and threats of their field division's WMD domain.

STATEMENT ON COMPLIANCE WITH LAWS AND REGULATIONS

As required by the *Government Auditing Standards* we tested, as appropriate given our audit scope and objectives, selected transactions, records, procedures, and practices, to obtain reasonable assurance that the Federal Bureau of Investigation's (FBI) management complied with federal laws and regulations for which noncompliance, in our judgment, could have a material effect on the results of our audit. The FBI's management is responsible for ensuring compliance with federal laws and regulations applicable to the FBI's weapons of mass destruction Coordinator program. In planning our audit, we identified the following laws and regulations that concerned the operations of the FBI and that were significant in the context of the audit objectives:

- 28 U.S.C. § 533

- 28 C.F.R. § 0.85

- Homeland Security Presidential Directive 5

- Homeland Security Presidential Directive 15 and its annexes.

- U.S. Department of Homeland Security National Response Framework

Our audit included examining, on a test basis, the FBI's compliance with the aforementioned laws and regulations that could have a material effect on the FBI's operations, through interviewing FBI personnel and conducting assessments of the WMD Coordinator efforts to prevent, prepare, and respond to WMD. Nothing came to our attention that caused us to believe that the FBI was not in compliance with the aforementioned laws and regulations.

STATEMENT ON INTERNAL CONTROLS

As required by the *Government Auditing Standards* we tested as appropriate, internal controls significant within the context of our audit objectives. A deficiency in an internal control exists when the design or operation of a control does not allow management or employees, in the normal course of performing their assigned functions, to timely prevent or detect the following: (1) impairments to the effectiveness and efficiency of operations, (2) misstatements in financial or performance information, or (3) violations of laws and regulations. Our evaluation of the Federal Bureau of Investigation's (FBI) internal controls was not made for the purpose of providing assurance on its internal control structure as a whole. The FBI's management is responsible for the establishment and maintenance of internal controls.

Through our audit testing, we did not identify any deficiencies in the FBI's internal controls that are significant within the context of the audit objectives and based upon the audit work performed that we believe would affect the FBI's ability to effectively and efficiently operate to correctly state financial and performance information and to ensure compliance with laws, regulations, and other applicable requirements.

Because we are not expressing an opinion on the FBI's internal control structure as a whole, this statement is intended solely for the information and use of the FBI. This restriction is not intended to limit the distribution of this report, which is a matter of public record.

DEFINITIONS

Domain is the territory and issues for which a field division or an FBI investigative program exercises responsibility or authority.

Domain Assessments are traditionally intelligence gathering and evaluation activities programmed to capture, review, and prioritize threats, vulnerabilities, and intelligence gaps presented by specific domain entities.

Domain Awareness is the knowledge of the prioritized domain threats and vulnerabilities that is acquired via domain assessments. When activities are planned and performed based on prioritized threats and vulnerabilities, a FBI field division or program achieves "true domain awareness."

Domain Entities are specific items or attributes of the domain. For the WMD domain, specific examples can range from specific people that have the knowledge or desire to obtain WMDs to security efforts at seaports and airports.

Domain Management is the process by which a field division manages and improves its domain awareness.

Field Divisions are the 56 FBI field offices and any resident agencies within their respective geographic area of responsibility.

Intelligence is information that has been analyzed, edited, and refined so that it is useful to policymakers and law enforcement personnel, especially in regard to national security threats.

Threats and Vulnerabilities are weaknesses, risks, and gaps that are assessed and prioritized by a domain assessment. Threats and vulnerabilities can range from those that pertain to a specific domain entity or to the entire domain.

ACRONYMS

CBRN	Chemical, Biological, Radiological, and Nuclear Material
CIA	Central Intelligence Agency
C.F.R.	Code of Federal Regulations
FBI	Federal Bureau of Investigation
HAZMAT	Hazardous Material
HSPD	Homeland Security Presidential Directive
IAS	Intelligence and Analysis Section
IIR	Intelligence Information Report
JTTF	Joint Terrorism Task Force
NSPD	National Security Presidential Directive
OIG	Office of the Inspector General
WMD	Weapons of Mass Destruction
SET	Strategic Execution Team Initiative
U.S.C.	United States Code

OBJECTIVES, SCOPE, AND METHODOLOGY

Objectives

The Department of Justice Office of the Inspector General (OIG) conducted an audit to: (1) assess how WMD Coordinators' should plan and perform activities that address prioritized WMD threats and vulnerabilities, (2) evaluate the FBI's integration of WMD Coordinator functions with field division intelligence capabilities and practices, and (3) review FBI efforts to ensure that WMD Coordinators and others that work on the WMD program have the skills and abilities necessary to detect and prevent WMD attacks.

Scope and Methodology

We conducted this performance audit in accordance with generally accepted government auditing standards. Those standards require that we plan and perform the audit to obtain sufficient, appropriate evidence to provide a reasonable basis for our findings and conclusions based on our audit objectives. We believe that the evidence obtained provides a reasonable basis for our findings and conclusions based on our audit objectives. The audit generally covers, but is not limited to, FBI WMD programs and activities from July 2006 to December 2008.

To accomplish our audit objectives, we obtained and reviewed all identified laws and regulations, as well as any other pertinent internal WMD program policies and guidance. In conducting this audit we interviewed over 80 FBI officials and employees, including the Assistant Director of the WMD Directorate. To obtain background in the field division WMD program and understand the environment that WMD Coordinators work in, we also attended the WMD Coordinators Conference in Albuquerque, New Mexico in June 2008. At the conference, we observed examples of training provided to WMD Coordinators.

We conducted field work and interviewed FBI officials and personnel with its WMD Directorate, the Directorate of Intelligence, and other pertinent operational groups at FBI headquarters in Washington, D.C. We also visited and spoke to officials and personnel at eight FBI field divisions. Our selection of the field divisions was based on a methodology that considered various aspects of WMD activities, intelligence and operational capabilities, liaison and other contacts with industry, academia, and emergency response groups, as well as field division size and geographical disparity.

SELECTED FIELD DIVISION SITES

Houston, Texas	New York, New York
Oklahoma City, Oklahoma	Phoenix, Arizona
Baltimore, Maryland	Tampa, Florida
Washington, D.C.	Los Angeles, California

Source: OIG assessment of WMD data

Because the FBI considers the WMD Coordinator the field division subject matter expert on WMD, we conducted interviews with WMD Coordinators, their supervisors, and other managers to determine the methodology and requirements for selecting such agents for the position. We also assessed WMD Coordinator performance plans and related activities to determine whether the performance plans adequately address their activities and allow them to be rated on a fair set of metrics.

Further, our audit work included many interviews with FBI private industry liaison partners, public health agencies, and state and local police departments. Our audit also included discussions and interviews with officials at other federal agencies, including the U.S. Department of Homeland Security and the U.S. Department of State. Officials and personnel with these organizations provided their input on the interaction with the field division WMD Coordinators and the types of training and information received from FBI officials, including WMD Coordinators and their assistants.

Domain Management

Throughout the audit, the methods by which field divisions evaluated and performed field division WMD program activities changed in response to the FBI's implementation of domain management. Recognizing these changes, we adjusted our audit objectives during our review to ensure that we assessed how the FBI's application of domain management to field division WMD programs would affect the WMD Coordinator's role. We then used the results of our fieldwork to determine what we believe are best practices that the FBI needs to implement to sustain a comprehensive WMD domain management process at its field divisions. Because the FBI only began to apply the domain concept to its field division WMD programs during our audit, we could not evaluate the results of its implementation of its process.

To identify the types of activities performed by WMD Coordinators, we also relied upon information contained in reports submitted by WMD Coordinators to FBI headquarters on a periodic basis that are used to summarize statistical accomplishment information at the field division level. We analyzed this information to determine the type of categories that are captured and reported and to identify whether WMD Coordinator activities were adequate to address the field division WMD threats and vulnerabilities. We reviewed planned updates to these reports. We also assessed the field division and FBI headquarters WMD incident response framework, including guidance, and analyzed the number of threats per field division and related threat assessments.

We collected, reviewed, and assessed each field division's WMD Semi-Annual Program Review as they were performed and completed during our audit. Each field division identified and listed their top WMD threats on their Semi-Annual Program Review. We conducted interviews with field division WMD Coordinators to ascertain how they identified and prioritized these threats. Because the FBI had not ensured that WMD Coordinators knew of the domain management approach, the WMD Coordinators were not able to use domain awareness to identify their field division's top threats on the Semi-Annual Program Review.

Intelligence and Strategic Execution Teams

We determined the adequacy of field division analytical support by conducting interviews and reviewing documentation to assess whether the WMD program has a designated Intelligence Analyst. We also reviewed the related activity level of field division Intelligence Analysts to determine whether their time was adequately allocated to support the WMD program at the field division. We reviewed the different types of intelligence reports at the field division level and assessed the differences among them. Such reports included Intelligence Information Reports, Intelligence Bulletins, and Intelligence Assessments. We also reviewed the field division's most recent Semi-Annual Program Review, to determine the field divisions' assessment of analytical support.

The FBI also established Strategic Execution Teams (SET) and continued restructuring the Field Intelligence Groups during the audit. To assess the impact of SET on field division WMD programs, we reviewed FBI policies and guidance related to the FBI's reorganization of their Intelligence Groups as carried out by the Strategic Execution Teams, obtained and analyzed pertinent supporting documentation, and conducted interviews to assess how these changes could impact the WMD program at the field division level. During these interviews, we took into consideration the early status of its field division intelligence reorganization at the field divisions and the schedule of SET implementation from March 2008 to January 2009.

Training

We obtained lists from the FBI documenting their assigned WMD Coordinators and Intelligence Analysts. We also pulled assignments for these positions from different WMD related training attendance lists. We identified and reviewed the various types of training opportunities that are available to WMD Coordinators, Assistant Coordinators, Intelligence Analysts, and other WMD personnel outside the FBI. We collected all designated WMD Coordinators and Intelligence Analysts training records from the FBI's Virtual Academy System. We relied on this computer generated data as it was pulled from the official training system used by the FBI. Therefore we did not conduct testing to verify the accuracy of this data from the Virtual Academy system. We analyzed the training received by WMD Coordinators and Intelligence Analysts and compared that to the modalities of WMD to determine the percentage of WMD Coordinators and Intelligence Analysts that have had some form of modality-based training.

A review of WMD Coordinator training records in the FBI's Virtual Academy system showed that, as of October 2008, just over half have recorded basic WMD training. As shown below, our analysis also revealed that WMD Coordinators have recorded limited training on specific WMD modalities.[33]

---

[33] We consider the major components or modalities of WMD to include biological, chemical, radiological, nuclear, and agro terrorism. To complete this analysis we broke WMD Coordinator training into eight common WMD modalities which can be defined as the following: (1) General WMD or CBRN; (2) Biological; (3) Chemical, including chemical explosives; (4) Radiological; (5) Nuclear; (6) Agro-terrorism; (7) Explosives; and (8) Hazardous Materials. We recognize that additional training may have been received prior to joining the FBI; however, this training has not been analyzed as part of this review.

PERCENTAGE OF WMD COORDINATORS THAT HAD RECEIVED WMD TRAINING AS OF OCTOBER 2008

WMD Modality	Percent of WMD Coordinators that Received Training[*]
WMD	58 percent
Agro-terrorism	51 percent
Biological	47 percent
Chemical	28 percent
Radiological	25 percent
Nuclear	7 percent
Explosives	70 percent
Hazardous Materials	53 percent

Source: OIG Analysis of FBI official training records
* Calculation based on total 57 WMD Coordinators.

Intelligence Analysts that worked with WMD Coordinators told us that they did not have a strong WMD background or knowledgebase and also lacked substantive training on WMD modalities, such as chemical, biological, radiological, or nuclear disciplines. We reviewed FBI Intelligence Analyst training records and found that few received specialized WMD modality courses as shown below.

WMD INTELLIGENCE ANALYST TRAINING

WMD Modality	WMD Intelligence Analysts Participating*
Domestic or International Terrorism	88 percent
WMD Intelligence Analyst Conference	88 percent
Agro-terrorism	15 percent
Biological	13 percent
Chemical	5 percent
Radiological	0 percent
Nuclear	5 percent
Explosives	5 percent
Hazardous Materials	7 percent
Counterproliferation	29 percent

Source: OIG Analysis of Virtual Academy Records

* Note: Calculation based upon 86 analysts, which includes one analyst position for all field divisions regardless of whether they had one designated as well as multiple Analysts that were designated at field divisions. (Number of Analysts Trained/86)

Although we assessed WMD Coordinator and Intelligence Analyst training as provided from Virtual Academy, we recognize that many weaknesses exist in the system. Training in WMD Modality areas could have been obtained from outside sources, including the CIA and other U.S. Intelligence Community partners, however is not included and tracked in Virtual Academy. We also recognize that additional training may have been received prior to joining the FBI; however, this training has not been analyzed as part of this review. Because of these recognized weaknesses, we could not rely on this assessment of training and could not determine whether the assessment actually reflects the training status of WMD employees. Therefore we did not include this assessment as a condition in the related finding.

Other Items

Throughout the audit, explored all identified, ongoing initiatives at the WMD Directorate that related to the field division WMD Coordinators and Intelligence Analysts, including domain assessment pilot programs, case reviews and templates used, and additional systems that are being built or designed to facilitate WMD readiness. We conducted interviews to obtain additional information on the Training Readiness Management System and Domain Liaison Knowledgebase, and we received and reviewed documentation pertaining to these systems. The Training Readiness Management System is used by the Hostage Rescue Team and Critical Incident Response Group, and the Domain Liaison Knowledgebase is used by the Counterintelligence Division.

OVERVIEW OF INVESTIGATIVE RESPONSIBILITIES OF THE FBI'S NATIONAL SECURITY BRANCH

The FBI assigns each investigation a case classification number that depends on the nature of the crime or activity being investigated. Accordingly, each division of the National Security Branch has been assigned to lead or act as the case manager for a particular set of case classification numbers. For example, the Counterterrorism Division manages most domestic and international investigations into terrorist activities while the Counterintelligence Division manages espionage, foreign intelligence, and country-threat counterproliferation investigations.

NATIONAL SECURITY BRANCH
CASE CLASSIFICATION RESPONSIBILITIES

Investigative Division	Case Type	Number of Lead Investigative Responsibilities
Counterintelligence	Espionage, Foreign Political Matters, Specified Country Proliferation, Assets, Students	293
Counterterrorism	Preparedness for Special Events, Aviation, Assets, International Terrorism, Overthrow/Destruction of Government	105
WMD Directorate	Threat, attempt, use, possess, produce, transfer WMD, and Develop or use Nuclear Materials and facilities in the U.S.	8

Source: FBI

The Counterterrorism and Counterintelligence Divisions may therefore administer types of cases that have a WMD connection. For example, a case involving domestic terrorism may include an investigation into how a suspect or target can acquire a WMD device. Although the Counterterrorism Division would lead the case, FBI officials told us that the designated agents in the field division or at the Directorate would be notified and assist Counterterrorism agents with the WMD portion of the investigation. Therefore, because the lead investigative division maintains responsibility for its cases, even if a WMD issue is revealed in a non-WMD case, the lead investigative agency would still manage day-to-day case activity. In such an instance, the WMD Directorate's role would be to assist Special Agents by providing subject matter expertise with the WMD portion of the other investigative division's case.

Although the WMD Directorate supports all terrorism investigations that have a connection to WMD, in April 2008, the FBI established new case classifications to facilitate its WMD mission and transferred certain case classifications to the WMD sub-program.

THE WMD INTELLIGENCE REPORTING PROCESS

Under FBI intelligence reporting guidelines, Intelligence Information Reports (IIRs) are drafted by Special Agents or Intelligence Analysts and submitted to a Chief Reports Officer, who assesses whether it complies with intelligence requirements and other standards. The Chief Reports Officer also may solicit input from field division leadership before submitting a draft IIR to the Report's Section at the Directorate of Intelligence. Analysts at the Directorate of Intelligence then review the draft IIRs, with input from headquarters level units such as the WMD Directorate, to ensure that it contains only accurate and relevant information.[34] Should these analysts question information presented by the draft IIR or otherwise need to revise it, they will send the submitting field division a note documenting why they did not disseminate the IIR and suggest how it can be modified to meet intelligence requirements.

The speed at which the Directorate of Intelligence needs to review IIRs is determined by its designation at either the immediate, priority, or routine precedence levels. Immediate IIRs contain information that is specific and extremely time sensitive and the Directorate of Intelligence has 24 hours from receipt to approve and disseminate the IIR. Priority IIRs are also time sensitive; however the information they contain does not warrant an immediate review. Priority IIRs must be reviewed and disseminated within five business days after receipt. Routine IIR information is of interest to the larger U.S. Intelligence Community, but their information is not time sensitive. The Directorate of Intelligence has 10 business days to review routine IIRs.

Once draft IIRs are reviewed at the program, field, and headquarters level, they are disseminated out of the FBI to relevant members of the U.S. Intelligence Community. While the intelligence production apparatus includes several stages of review, the collaboration on intelligence reporting ensures that accurate information is provided to the U.S. Intelligence Community. Such collaboration also serves to encourage special agents and Intelligence Analysts, as well as their units, to engage and communicate toward a common intelligence objective.

---

[34] The analysis of FBI field division intelligence is facilitated by the FBI's Human Intelligence Program that guides the acquisition and maintenance of people to serve as intelligence sources. As a part of its review, the Directorate of Intelligence evaluates the nature and validity of information acquired from human sources, and if necessary, translates or interprets such information.

WMD CONTINUING HIGHER EDUCATION PROGRAM
COURSE CATALOG

Phase 1: WMD Master's Certificate Program Courses

1. Criminological Theory – Examination of theories with emphasis on approaches to crime and criminally deviant behavior

2. Pro Seminar – Survey of current research and critical issues. For FBI, emphasis on infrastructure threat assessments and protections; utilization of Sandia National laboratory subject matter experts

3. Hazardous Materials Management – Examines technical and management aspects of handling hazardous materials and reviews current trends. For FBI, emphasis is placed on the tracking of Hazmat versus the disposal of Hazmat, and discussions and review of policies and procedures

4. Disaster Preparedness – Principles and techniques for preparing for various types of disasters. For FBI, emphasis is on the impact to and by law enforcement in disaster preparedness

5. Criminology Course – Capstone course to integrate all portions of certificate program and complete a final project which addresses issues relevant to the FBI's mission in WMD.

Phase 2: WMD Master's Degree Completion Program Courses

1. Legal Issues in Criminology – In-depth study of contemporary legal issues faced by criminal justice professions. For the FBI, emphasis is on laws surrounding WMD.

2. Ethical and Philosophical Issues in Criminology – Intensive examination of selected ethical and philosophical issues currently facing the field of criminology. For FBI, emphasis is on ethical issues surrounding terrorism and WMD prosecutions; detentions and or prosecutions-traditional, enemy combatant, and other country restrictions or lack thereof.

3. Research Methods – Methods and techniques of research in criminology. For the FBI, emphasis is on research area critical to WMD strategy and execution.

4. Quantitative Strategies for Analysis in Criminology – Computer analysis of quantitative data to the behavior science of criminology. For the FBI, emphasis is on terrorism and WMD aspects and critiques of terrorism and WMD research.

5. Capstone Project – Brings all components of the Masters Program courses together to be presented and defended.

FBI RESPONSE TO THE DRAFT REPORT

U.S. Department of Justice

Federal Bureau of Investigation

Washington, D. C. 20535-0001

September 11, 2009

Mr. Raymond J. Beaudet
Assistant Inspector General for Audits
United States Department of Justice
Suite 6100
1425 New York Avenue, NW
Washington, DC 20530

RE: THE FEDERAL BUREAU OF INVESTIGATION'S WEAPONS OF MASS
DESTRUCTION COORDINATOR PROGRAM

Dear Mr. Beaudet:

The Federal Bureau of Investigation (FBI) appreciates the opportunity to review
and respond to your report entitled, "The Federal Bureau of Investigation's Weapons of Mass
Destruction Coordinator Program" (hereinafter, "Report"). The Report acknowledges and
highlights a number of effective FBI WMD program activities and responsibilities.

We are pleased the Office of the Inspector General recognizes the importance of
effective domain management by FBI WMD Coordinators within our field divisions, specifically
through the prioritization of WMD threats, vulnerabilities and interactions with FBI Intelligence
Analysts. The WMD Coordinators' functions are critical to the work of the FBI and its many law
enforcement, intelligence and public safety partners in countering the WMD threat. The FBI has
made strides to increase the competency of, and professionalize, our WMD Coordinators and
Intelligence Analysts through a formalized training curriculum and select performance
requirements. With regard to investigative management, including identification of WMD nexus
cases, management of investigative techniques, and coordination of investigative activities with
other related FBI investigative programs, the WMD Directorate has taken a forward leaning
approach toward cross-program integration. Namely, the WMD Directorate has embedded
Supervisory Special Agents and Intelligence Analysts into FBI Headquarters counterterrorism
case management units to identify cases with a WMD nexus and leverage WMD subject matter
expertise and resources, thus addressing those cases through a unique blend of investigative,
intelligence, scientific and technical perspectives. Overall this provides a direct benefit to the
WMD Coordinators and field office investigators ensuring comprehensive WMD
countermeasures, investigations and response operations.

Based on the review of the Report, the FBI concurs with the thirteen
recommendations to standardize WMD Coordinators' domain management responsibilities. By
implementing your recommendations the WMD Directorate will provide increased professional
opportunities and development for the WMD Coordinators and Intelligence Analysts who
prioritize WMD threats and coordinate activities within their respective domains. Through
collaboration with the Directorate of Intelligence, the WMD Directorate will implement various

Mr. Raymond J. Beaudet

procedures and practices to address intelligence exchange, performance, tracking and training relevant to effective domain management.

In conclusion, the FBI appreciates the professionalism exhibited by your staff in working with our representatives throughout this audit process. The FBI commends your committed support for the preeminent work of FBI WMD Coordinators and Intelligence Analysts in countering the global threat of WMD. Enclosed herein is the FBI's response to the report. Please feel free to contact me should you have any questions.

Sincerely yours,

Vahid Majidi, Ph.D.
Assistant Director
WMD Directorate

Enclosure

2

OIG Audit of the FBI's Weapons of Mass Destruction Threat Preparations FBI Response to Recommendations within the Final Draft

Recommendation 1: "Ensure that a WMD Coordinator or a designated assistant WMD Coordinator participates in their field division's WMD domain assessment"

FBI Response to Recommendation #1:

In August 2008, the Weapons of Mass Destruction Directorate (WMDD) initiated the WMD Domain Awareness Initiative. The WMD Intelligence Analysis Section (IAS) was tasked to formulate a set of protocols for the research, analysis, and production of WMD Domain Intelligence Notes. In addition, IAS was directed to manage the process, and the entire program was approved by WMDD and the Directorate of Intelligence's (DI's) Domain Section. The protocols included the involvement of field WMD Coordinators, particularly near the conclusion of the process when they would review the initial drafts and provide comment and feedback.

With the creation of the Central Strategic Coordinating Components (CSCC) in 2009 within each division's intelligence program, overall management and coordination of field WMD domain awareness will reside with the Intelligence Program Manager (IPM) and Intelligence Program Coordinator (IPC) in the CSCC. To ensure all field offices include the participation of WMD Coordinators, the WMD Directorate and CSCC will ensure participation through proactive contact with each field office executive management team and Field Intelligence Group (FIG).

Prior to submission of annual field office domain assessments, the CSCC will contact each FIG to reinforce the message that all WMD Coordinators need to be involved in the drafting of their WMD assessments. In addition, the CSCC will require each FIG to outline the steps taken to include their WMD Coordinator's involvement in the development and review of the assessment. The FIGs will be required to memorialize this in an Electronic Communication due no later than 31 January of each year.

Recommendation 2: "Develop procedures to ensure that field divisions regularly: (1) review cases for WMD connections and (2) share pertinent case information with appropriate personnel so it can be evaluated during WMD domain assessments"

FBI Response to Recommendation #2:

The IAS's Strategic Assessment and Threat Forecasting Unit (SATFU) has developed a Microsoft Access database template similar to the one referenced on page 23 of the OIG Draft Report. The SATFU template will be made available to all field divisions. When completed by the Case Agent, this template will highlight potential WMD links which should be brought to the attention of the WMD Coordinator and the WMDD. IAS will send guidance to all Joint Terrorism Task Force (JTTF) Supervisory Special Agents (SSAs), FIGs, and WMD Coordinators implementing the use of this database template and prompt notification to the WMD Coordinator regarding relevant links. Field offices will be required to send quarterly updates of the database to IAS. The data will then be posted on a Share Point site maintained by IAS and accessible by all FBI personnel.

The WMDD has mandated the use of standard FBI codes and indicators for all counterterrorism cases as a method of identifying those with a WMD nexus. FBIHQ oversight of these investigations ensures that field division personnel remain mindful of reviewing and properly classifying such cases for relevant links.

The above actions will ensure that field offices are reviewing their cases upon initiation, and quarterly thereafter, for connections to WMD matters. Access to the SATFU database by WMD Coordinators and the FIG will ensure that they and other appropriate personnel have access to this information for purposes such as the preparation of WMD domain assessments and the Semi-Annual Program Review (SAPR). These field office reviews will be in addition to the HQ-level case coordination between the WMDD and Counterterrorism Division which already exists and was noted by the OIG.

Recommendation 3: "Enhance the sharing of WMD domain entity information acquired by personnel working with outside groups."

FBI Response to Recommendation #3:

The WMDD is developing and deploying technological tools and solutions to address domain assessment and awareness. The WMD Coordinator, Domain Coordinator, and JTTF personnel will be able to access more information in order to update the field office WMD domain assessment.

WMDD has established information portals on the SECRET and TOP SECRET network enclaves using commercial off-the-shelf software accessible by all FBI personnel with access and a need to know. The latest threat, vulnerability, and countermeasures information from various internal and external sources is posted to the sites for use by WMD Coordinators. The portals serve as a cost effective method of communicating large amounts of information in a timely manner.

WMDD develops CBRNE-related workshops and conferences bringing together WMD Coordinators, Subject Matter Experts (SMEs), other federal, state and local agencies, and private entities to discuss current and emerging threats and vulnerabilities to domain entities. Examples of such conference and workshop initiatives include: The Joint FBI-EPA Regional Food and Agroterrorism Workshops, the Joint FBI-JTTF Water Terrorism Workshop, regional Improvised Explosives training, Clandestine Laboratory awareness training, joint FBI/CDC Criminal and Epidemiological Investigation Workshops, and regional Chemical Industry Outreach Workshops.

Specific domain identification and outreach efforts are to be documented and provided to the WMDD. The WMDD also requested notification of resulting identifiable accomplishment, detections, disruptions, investigations, sources, etc. The FBI has partnered with other federal agencies to conduct a series of CBRNE Tabletop Exercises to improve coordination of incident response and to prevent potential WMD incidents.

Policies are currently under review and will be approved shortly by WMDD to direct field WMD Coordinators to coordinate with other field office Program Coordinators within their offices to regularly share WMD domain information acquired through the above mentioned activities and initiatives across programs.

Recommendation 4: "Ensure that WMD Coordinators submit activity reports at regular intervals to facilitate tracking activities against domain needs."

FBI Response to Recommendation #4:

As noted in the OIG Draft Report, WMD Coordinators already submit activity reports to WMDD on an ad hoc basis, such as following a significant event or when prompted by FBIHQ in response to a data call by outside groups. In accordance with the recommendations of the OIG, WMDOU will set policy mandating that these reports be submitted to WMDOU every six months to cover activities conducted during the three months following the end of the previous SAPR period. This will require WMD Coordinators to remain focused on their divisions' needs and to report their activities to HQ at least once per quarter. The FD-542 statistical accomplishment macro in Word Perfect (version dated 03/23/2009) has been modified to capture a wider range of WMD-related activities and is therefore better suited than previous revisions to serve as the reporting document.

To ensure that activities are being conducted in support of a field division's individual domain needs, WMDOU will instruct WMD Coordinators to list and number these needs within the first paragraph of the narrative section of the FD-542 activity report. The subsequent activities can then be correlated to the particular domain need or needs which they address. WMDD also notes that sections II, III, IV, and VI of the most recent version of the SAPR deal with the WMD Domain Assessment and already require that the WMD Coordinator describe how his/her activities address the division's identified threats, vulnerabilities, and gaps.

WMD Coordinators will continue submitting activity reports following significant events and training exercises, or at other times deemed appropriate.

Recommendation 5: "Require that the WMD Directorate track WMD Coordinator activities against specific WMD domain threats and vulnerabilities to ensure that each field division is adequately managing its WMD domain."

FBI Response to Recommendation #5:

The FD-542 activity reports and SAPR's submitted in accordance with current policies and those to be enacted pursuant to OIG recommendation #4 above will be received and tracked by WMDOU. SSAs assigned to the WMDOU will continue to provide feedback to the WMD Coordinators regarding the effectiveness and relevance of their activities to their division's identified threats, vulnerabilities, and gaps.

Recommendation 6: "Develop performance-rating plans for the WMD Coordinator position based on the tasks and skills necessary to manage the WMD domain effectively."

FBI Response to Recommendation #6:

Due to their official position descriptions and job classification, WMDCs are bound by the current FBI Performance Appraisal System (PAS) metrics for the Special Agent (SA) job family (FD-727.2, Rev. 06-01-2006). The focus of these metrics is on efficient, innovative, and capable application of decision making, organizing and planning, analyzing, maintaining professional standards, acquiring and sharing job knowledge, achieving results and communicating effectively. These metrics for the SA also translate and apply to how effectively the WMD Coordinator is performing their duties. The WMDD therefore assess WMD Coordinator performance through the use of the SAPR and activity reports, as described in conjunction with OIG recommendation #4. WMDOU will evaluate the effectiveness of a division's WMD program as a whole, with the recognition that the program's success is largely dependent upon the collaboration of the WMD Coordinator with Intelligence Analysts and other investigative personnel within their divisional territory.

Recommendation 7: "Require that each field division designate an Intelligence Analyst to meet with the WMD Coordinator periodically and discuss their planned work and activities and provide feedback on whether these activities will address prioritized domain needs."

FBI Response to Recommendation #7:

An integrated workflow between field office Intelligence Analysts and WMD Coordinators is vital to ensure each field office is adequately assessing and prioritizing their domain needs. The WMDD will pursue the designation of part time, and full time analytical resources in each field office where possible, in order to provide central points of contact and facilitate WMD related analysis. The WMDD will collaborate with the DI to implement this designation over the next two years. The DI is the principal entity responsible for Intelligence Analyst career development and management.

In the interim, the WMD Intelligence Program will draft a current list of each field office's Intelligence Analyst(s) capable of working on WMD-related issues. This list will be updated on a six-month basis and posted on the WMD Intelligence Program SharePoint site. The WMDD will also post an updated and current list of each field office's WMD Coordinators. These lists will help field office personnel identify with whom in their divisions they should be working on WMD matters.

In addition, each field office FIG will be required to outline its analyst and coordinator integration on a periodic basis through Electronic Communication. Each FIG will memorialize on a quarterly basis the steps and efforts taken by Intelligence Analysts and WMD Coordinators to discuss their planned work and activities. These Electronic Communications will provide the basis for WMDD assessment of how well each field office is doing in enabling analyst-coordinator collaboration on WMD matters.

Recommendation 8: "Permit WMD Coordinators to consider purchases requested by designated WMD Intelligence Analysts in formulating their field division WMD budget requests."

FBI Response to Recommendation #8:

To help facilitate appropriate purchases of WMD materials by field Intelligence Analysts, the WMDD will work through established DI channels. Functionally, all budget related requisitions and requests for Intelligence Analysts fall under the DI, the WMDD recognizes the importance of this issue.

The WMDCU has made available to every WMD Coordinator reference materials, books, and other educational documents. During Fiscal Year 2010 WMDCU will continue disseminating such material to all field offices. These materials will be intended for consumption by WMD Intelligence Analysts as well as Coordinators. To better inform all field office personnel of materials available, WMDD will disseminate information concerning these materials on an annual basis to all FBI FIGs. WMD Intelligence Analysts will be encouraged to work with Coordinators to obtain materials and make special or official requests for additional needs through the DI and the WMDD.

Recommendation 9: "Develop and disseminate WMD Coordinator position qualifications to field division management and WMD Coordinators to use in appointing future WMD Coordinators and for delineating the necessary skills and abilities current WMD Coordinators should obtain."

FBI Response to Recommendation #9:

The FBI identifies and tracks select new agents with a WMD Specialty Designation based on relevant educational background and/or work experience.

The WMD Specialty Designation is a sub-specialty that can be applied to any agent regardless of their designated career path (i.e. criminal, counterintelligence, counterterrorism, cyber, intelligence). Any WMD training opportunities will be provided under the auspice of the WMDD's Developmental Plan (see page 14).

The above criteria used to select and train new agents for the WMD Specialty Designation are also applicable to the selection and training of experienced SAs under consideration to fill vacancies in WMD Coordinator (or Alternate) positions. WMDOU will send an electronic communication to all field divisions directing that this criterion be used as guidance when considering WMD Coordinator (or Alternate) candidates. Personnel filling those roles will also be required to attend the courses mandated under Phase Two of the WMDD's Developmental Plan within one year of assuming the position, and encouraged to complete the path to full certification.

Recommendation 10: "Develop and implement a method that shares and reconciles Training Readiness Management System data with Virtual Academy records."

FBI Response to Recommendation #10:

The purpose of Virtual Academy is to maintain training records for all FBI employees; to create a system for training registration and approval; and to provide a portal for accessing Web-based training. The purpose of WMDD Training Readiness Management System (TRMS) is to track the readiness of individual FBI employees and of aggregate entities (e.g. field offices or regions) to address WMD threats. For this purpose, individual readiness has been defined as the extent to which an individual employee has completed the WMD training mandated by WMDD given the employee's job function and the length of time the employee has occupied a WMD role. For an aggregate entity, readiness has been defined as a weighted average of the readiness scores of the tracked employees within the aggregate entity. In order to calculate readiness scores, TRMS contains data on all WMD-related courses offered inside and outside of the FBI completed by the tracked employees, ultimately contributing to aggregate readiness scores. TRMS also has ancillary capabilities, i.e. the ability to determine how proposed future training would impact aggregate readiness scores thus allowing WMDD to provide new courses positively impacting readiness levels.

The missions of Virtual Academy and TRMS are different. There is a limited and well-defined subset of data common to both systems; training records for WMD-related courses. These records are in Virtual Academy and exported to TRMS. WMD-related courses offered by the FBI are entered into TRMS from the Virtual Academy. Virtual Academy does not currently capture training records for courses offered outside the FBI. Therefore, to successfully track WMD training outside the FBI, these courses must be entered into the WMDD TRMS through SharePoint. The Virtual Academy Unit is completing the development of a Self-Reported Training function to capture training outside the FBI. When deployed, the Virtual Academy will become the sole source of course data for TRMS.

Recommendation 11: "Finalize its WMD Coordinator certification program opportunities and ensure that the finalized certification program offers threat-based courses based on the WMD domain threats and vulnerabilities within a WMD Coordinator's field division."

FBI Response to Recommendation #11:

WMDD National Preparedness Unit (NPU), in conjunction with the Human Resource Division/Special Agent Career Path Unit, has established a series of WMD specific courses, exercises and on-the-job requirements for individuals to be certified in the WMD Specialty area. WMD training opportunities are provided under the auspice of the WMDD's Developmental Plan (see page 14). The WMDD Developmental Plan is devised in conjunction with the WMD Specialty Designation for new agents (WMD Specialty Agents); WMD Coordinators will be required and Assistant WMD Coordinators are encouraged to apply for certification.

Currently, the WMDD's Developmental Plan outlines four stages of WMD development. Stage One involves an elementary level of WMD training, which is provided to all new agents at the FBI Academy in Quantico, VA. Stage Two involves additional introductory WMD training an Agent can pursue post Quantico. Stage Three involves specialized and intermediate levels of WMD training, as well as acquisition of experience in handling WMD. Upon successful completion of Stage Three, interested agents are encouraged to submit an application via EC to the WMD Certification Review Board where the applicant must provide information on WMD on-the-job training or experience, WMD training they received and provided as instructors, along with a synopsis of why they are interested in receiving WMD Certification.

The WMD Certification Board will then review these applications on a semi-annual basis. The WMD Certification Review Board will consist of the following representatives: 1 Unit Chief (non-voting chairperson) from WMD Operations Unit (WMDOU) or WMD National Preparedness Unit (WMDNPU), 1 SSA from WMDOU; 1 SSA from WMDNPU; 1 SSA or Hazardous Materials Officer from the Hazardous Materials Response Unit; and 4 WMD Coordinators (WMDC) from the field. WMDOU will select the WMDCs who participate. WMDOU will select one WMDC from each geographic region managed by WMDOU (i.e. Northeast, Southeast, Central, West). Upon each successful review of applications by the WMD Certification Review Board, NPU will notify agents via EC whether they will receive WMD Certification.

Agents who complete the WMD Certification process will receive the following:

- Certificate signed by the Assistant Director of the WMDD
- Consideration in WMD Specialty Transfers
- Consideration in SSA Positions in the WMDD at FBIHQ
- Peer Recognition

Recommendation 12: "Implement a procedure by which the courses offered by the Indiana University of Pennsylvania Masters Certificate Program and Masters Degree Completion Program are regularly reviewed and assessed to ensure that course material address the changing needs of WMD Coordinators and Intelligence Analysts."

FBI Response to Recommendation #12:

Upon completion of each course sequence, students have been queried by the FBI Program Manager to ensure the course materials address current areas of concern for WMD personnel. At least once a quarter, NPU personnel meet with the Indiana University of Pennsylvania (IUP) Faculty Program Manager, IUP Research Institute personnel, and other IUP Faculty members as needed, to review and modify (if necessary) the curriculum within the boundaries of the university's accreditation standards. Between meetings, the FBI Program Manager maintains regular contact with IUP faculty and staff to ensure the program remains on track and meets the needs of the WMDD. This process has been in place since the inception of the program.

Based upon the recommendations from the participants in the two initial cohorts (course iterations), the following changes have been implemented:

- Delivery of the textbooks and the course syllabus to the participants a few weeks in advance of the course start dates to allow participants to read ahead and begin course assignments prior to the start of the course

- Brief the IUP faculty members regarding the participants' backgrounds to prevent them from covering material already know by the participants (e.g. Incident Command System (ICS) and National Incident Management System (NIMS))

- Change the sequence of the courses to allow for more logical progression of the course work

- Survey of current and over-the-horizon threats to make sure the course curriculum stays relevant

Recommendation 13: "Develop a targeted WMD training plan encompassing both general and specific WMD-knowledge requirements for Intelligence Analysts who work with WMD Coordinators that address the specific vulnerabilities."

FBI Response to Recommendation #13:

The WMDD has ongoing efforts to assist field office personnel—both WMD Coordinators and Intelligence Analysts. WMDD's Countermeasures Unit has encouraged field offices to provide funding to send their coordinators and analysts to all WMDD-approved training opportunities. WMDD's National Preparedness Unit has also made WMDD Special Agent Career Path (SACP) courses accessible to field office Intelligence Analysts working WMD-related matters. SACP courses are threat-based courses that are aligned with the national threats, priorities, and goals.

All Intelligence Analyst training is managed by the DI and the WMDD will work with the DI's Intelligence Training Coordination Unit to develop a field office WMD Intelligence Analyst curriculum of required and elective WMD courses offered by FBI and other US Government agencies. The WMD Intelligence Program will complete its internal list of required and elective courses by 31 December 2009, and this list will be provided to ITCU to help formulate a targeted training plan for field office Intelligence Analysts.

OIG SUMMARY AND ANALYSIS OF ACTIONS NECESSARY TO CLOSE REPORT

The OIG provided a draft of this report to the FBI, and the FBI's response to the report recommendations is included in Appendix V. In addition, the FBI provided the OIG an addendum to its formal response that it considered law enforcement sensitive because it detailed specific activities planned or undertaken to address recommendations 2, 3, and 9. This addendum is not included in this report, but we considered this information in assessing the status of these recommendations. The following provides the OIG analysis of the FBI's response and a summary of actions necessary to close the report.

Summary of Actions Necessary to Close the Report

1. **Resolved.** The FBI concurred with our recommendation to ensure that a WMD Coordinator or a designated assistant WMD Coordinator participates in their field division's WMD domain assessment. The FBI recently created the Central Strategic Coordinating Components (CSCC) within each division's intelligence program and reported that overall management and coordination of field WMD domain awareness will reside with the CSCC. The FBI reported that, prior to the submission of annual field office domain assessments, the CSCC will contact each Field Intelligence Group to ensure that WMD Coordinators are involved in the WMD assessment process. The CSCC will require each Field Intelligence Group to outline and report annually the steps taken to include WMD Coordinators in the development and review of the domain assessment. This recommendation can be closed when the FBI provides evidence that its WMD Coordinators work with Field Intelligence Groups in the domain assessments process.

2. **Resolved.** We recommended that the FBI develop procedures to ensure that field offices regularly: (1) review cases for WMD connections and (2) share pertinent case information with appropriate personnel so it can be evaluated during WMD domain assessments. The FBI concurred with our recommendation and stated that it is developing a database template for its field offices to highlight potential WMD links in cases. According to the FBI, these links will then be brought to the attention of both the WMD Coordinator and the WMD Directorate.

The FBI also responded that it will issue guidance to its Joint Terrorism Task Forces, Supervisory Special Agents, Field Intelligence Groups, and WMD Coordinators to ensure that these groups and officials use this database template and notify the WMD Coordinator when they identify relevant WMD links. The FBI is also requiring that its field offices send quarterly database updates to FBI Headquarters, thereby ensuring that field divisions are reviewing their cases regularly for WMD connections. This recommendation can be closed when the FBI provides copies of (1) the database template and (2) the guidance it provided to its Joint Terrorism Task Forces, Supervisory Special Agents, Field Intelligence Groups, and WMD Coordinators regarding the proper use of the database template.

3.   **Resolved.** We recommended that the FBI enhance the sharing of WMD domain entity information acquired by personnel working with outside groups. The FBI concurred with this recommendation and reported that it is continuing to develop new tools to enhance updating and sharing of WMD domain entity information. For example, the FBI said it is developing applications for WMD Coordinators to use in displaying domain entities and classified information portals that can be used to post the up-to-date information on threats, vulnerabilities, and countermeasures. In addition, the FBI is developing WMD-related workshops, conferences, and tabletop exercises with outside entities.

The FBI has also directed its field offices to provide the WMD Directorate the results of any outreach with certain types of domain entities. In its response, the FBI further advised that it is developing policies that will ensure that WMD Coordinators work with other field office personnel to share WMD domain information. This recommendation can be closed when the FBI provides (1) evidence that field offices are reporting relevant outreach results to the WMD Directorate and (2) copies of the issued policies directing WMD Coordinators to coordinate and share information with other coordinators in their field offices.

4.   **Resolved.** The FBI concurred with our recommendation to ensure that WMD Coordinators submit activity reports at regular intervals to facilitate tracking their activities against domain needs. The FBI reports that it has updated the standard activity report format to capture additional WMD Coordinator activities and will mandate that WMD Coordinators submit these activity reports on a regular basis. To ensure that WMD Coordinator activities are being conducted in support of a field division's unique domain needs, the FBI will require that the

WMD Coordinators identify their domain needs in their standard activity report.

This recommendation can be closed when the FBI provides (1) a copy of the updated activity report format that WMD Coordinators use to report their activities, (2) a copy of the policy that mandates regular activity report submissions, and (3) evidence that WMD Coordinators use activity reports to detail their activities for comparison against identified domain needs.

5. **Resolved.** We recommended that the FBI require that its WMD Directorate track WMD Coordinator activities against specific WMD domain threats and vulnerabilities to ensure that each field division is adequately managing its WMD domain. The FBI agreed with this recommendation and stated that the WMD Directorate will use the updated activity report format that includes domain information to provide feedback to WMD Coordinators and ensure that they address domain threats and vulnerabilities. This recommendation can be closed when the FBI provides evidence that (1) WMD Coordinators are submitting activity reports on a regular basis and (2) the WMD Directorate is using this information to track WMD Coordinator activities against specific WMD domain threats and vulnerabilities.

6. **Resolved.** We recommended that the FBI develop performance-rating plans for the WMD Coordinator position based on the tasks and skills necessary to manage their WMD domains effectively. In its response, the FBI concurred with the recommendation but advised that under its current agency-wide performance appraisal system WMD Coordinators must be rated as Special Agents. Therefore, while the FBI cannot develop performance rating plans for the WMD Coordinator position, the FBI stated that it will use Special Agent metrics – namely whether a Special Agent is efficient, innovative, and capable of decision making, organizing and planning, analyzing, maintaining professional standards, acquiring and sharing job knowledge, achieving results, and communicating effectively – to assess WMD Coordinator performance.

The FBI also stated that it will actively assess the overall effectiveness of each field division's WMD program by reviewing results of Semi-Annual Program Reviews and the updated WMD Coordinator activity reports. This recommendation is resolved based on the FBI's plans to assess both WMD Coordinator and WMD program performance at each field division. This recommendation can be closed once the FBI provides evidence that its assessments of each field division's WMD program are consistently considered and used by field office managers and supervisors to help rate individual WMD Coordinator performance that use Special Agent metrics.

7. **Resolved.** We recommended that the FBI require each field division to designate an Intelligence Analyst to meet with the WMD Coordinator periodically to discuss planned work and activities and provide feedback on whether these activities will address prioritized domain needs. The FBI agreed with this recommendation and stated that it is working to designate analytical resources at each field office. The FBI also stated that its WMD Directorate is taking immediate steps to ensure that WMD Coordinators can identify who at each field office can provide them WMD intelligence support.

This recommendation can be closed when the FBI provides the OIG: (1) copies of any guidance made available to WMD Coordinators that identifies the Intelligence Analysts capable of working on WMD-related issues, (2) copies of field office reports on designating Field Intelligence Group resources to work with WMD Coordinators, and (3) evidence that it has formalized and implemented an agency-wide solution that ensures collaboration on WMD matters between WMD Coordinators and field division Intelligence Analysts.

8. **Resolved.** We recommended that the FBI permit WMD Coordinators to consider purchases requested by designated WMD Intelligence Analysts in formulating their field office WMD budget requests. The FBI agreed with this recommendation and stated that it is working to facilitate purchases of material and equipment needed by Intelligence Analysts.

The FBI also stated that its WMD Directorate is providing reference materials, such as books and educational documents, to all field offices, which can be used by WMD Coordinators and Intelligence Analysts. To ensure that all Intelligence Analysts know that the each field division has WMD reference material, the FBI said it plans to inform its Field Intelligence Groups annually that the WMD Coordinator has these materials.

To close this recommendation, the FBI should provide evidence that its WMD Coordinators can consider the shared program needs offered by WMD-designated Intelligence Analysts in formulating their budgets and providing WMD–related materials for their field office. The annual advisement to Field Intelligence Groups regarding the availability of WMD reference materials should also provide WMD Coordinators and Intelligence Analysts an opportunity to request additional WMD-specific resources. Individual Intelligence Analysts could then make known a need for specific WMD material to the WMD Coordinator, who could then consider the request in formulating a budget or updating the WMD Directorate if this request addresses a potential agency-wide need. If the requested material primarily concerns intelligence or analytical capabilities, the WMD Coordinator or the WMD Directorate could then relay the request to Directorate of Intelligence for resolution.

9. **Resolved.** We recommended that the FBI develop and disseminate WMD Coordinator position qualifications to field division management and WMD Coordinators to use in appointing future WMD Coordinators and for delineating the necessary skills and abilities current WMD Coordinators should obtain. The FBI agreed and provided criteria used for purposes of selecting and training Special Agents for the WMD Specialty Designation. The FBI stated that these criteria will be used to select and train experienced Special Agents to fill WMD Coordinator vacancies.

The FBI also stated in its response that personnel who fill these positions will be required to complete certain courses within 1 year of assuming the position. This recommendation can be closed when the FBI provides the OIG a copy of the policy disseminated to all field offices regarding WMD Coordinator qualifications.

10. **Resolved.** We recommended that the FBI develop and implement a method that shares and reconciles Training Readiness Management System data with Virtual Academy records. While agreeing with the recommendation, the FBI emphasized that the missions of the Virtual Academy system and the Training Readiness Management System are different and, as a result, both capture a limited and well-defined subset of data – WMD training offered by the FBI. Therefore, the FBI stated that it is developing a self-reported training function that will allow Virtual Academy to capture non-FBI training.

The recommendation recognizes that the FBI's Virtual Academy system and its Training Readiness Management System will both capture and use a limited subset of data. Importantly, once Virtual Academy is adjusted to record and track non-FBI training, the amount of data shared between the two systems will increase. This recommendation therefore seeks to ensure that any shared data is complete and accurate. To close this recommendation, the FBI should provide evidence that once Virtual Academy is used to record non-FBI training, the FBI is using Virtual Academy training records to update relevant portions of its Training Readiness Management System.

11. **Resolved.** We recommended that the FBI finalize its WMD Coordinator certification program opportunities and ensure that the finalized certification program offers threat-based courses based on the WMD domain threats and vulnerabilities within a WMD Coordinator's field office. The FBI concurred with this recommendation and stated that the WMD Directorate has worked with the Human Resource Division to establish a series of WMD-specific courses, exercises, and on-the-job requirements for WMD certification. After completing certain WMD training courses, the FBI is encouraging Special Agents to apply for WMD Certification. According to the FBI, all WMD Coordinators will be required to apply for certification. This recommendation can be closed when the FBI provides evidence that (1) WMD Coordinators are applying for and maintaining WMD Certification, which thereby ensures that WMD Coordinators complete a certain level of WMD coursework; and (2) WMD Coordinators are receiving threat-based training aligned to field division WMD domain threats and vulnerabilities.

12. **Closed.** We recommended that the FBI implement a procedure by which the courses offered by the Indiana University of Pennsylvania Masters Certificate Program and Masters Degree Completion Program (Program) are regularly reviewed and assessed to ensure that course materials address the changing needs of WMD Coordinators and Intelligence Analysts. The FBI agreed and has instituted procedures that ensure that the Program meets the needs of the FBI's WMD personnel. For example, the FBI stated that after each course sequence it queries students to ensure that course material addressed their concerns. The FBI has also met and discussed the curriculum and necessary modifications with the Indiana University of Pennsylvania. The FBI provided a list of changes made within the program as a result of student queries and meetings with University personnel. Based on this evidence, the OIG considers this recommendation closed.

13. **Resolved.** We recommended that the FBI develop a targeted WMD training plan encompassing both general and specific WMD-knowledge requirements for Intelligence Analysts who work with WMD Coordinators. This plan should address the specific vulnerabilities and threats of a field division's WMD domain. The FBI concurred with the recommendation and is having its WMD Directorate work with its Directorate of Intelligence to develop a field office WMD Intelligence

95

Analyst curriculum. The FBI reported that a list of required and elective courses will be developed by December 31, 2009, and will be used to help formulate a targeted training plan for field office Intelligence Analysts. This recommendation can be closed when the FBI provides the OIG with a copy of the finalized targeted training plan for field office Intelligence Analysts who work with WMD Coordinators.